# A Retreat With
## Francis and Clare of Assisi
## *Following Our Pilgrim Hearts*

Murray Bodo and Susan Saint Sing

ST. ANTHONY MESSENGER PRESS

Cincinnati, Ohio

# Other titles in the
# A Retreat With... *Series:*

# Contents

Dedicated to the memory of
*FATHER AARON PEMBLETON, O.F.M.*
*1935-1995*
*pilgrim par excellence*
*who led pilgrims through Assisi's streets*
*every summer from 1974 to 1994*
*and*
*LOUIS BODO*
*1914-1996*
*whose fly rod*
*was his pilgrimage*
*and retreat*

## Acknowledgments

We would like to thank Sister Dianne Short, O.S.C., for contributing to the reflection questions for each day of the retreat, and Sister Bernice Stenger, O.S.F., for her careful reading of the manuscript. We are grateful to both for their helpful suggestions, as well.

We would also like to thank our publishing family at St. Anthony Messenger Press, all those who have worked on our books over the years, the publishers, editors, proofreaders, publicists, designers, typists, printers; those who make the paper and ink for the books, those who take orders for books, who box and mail them, those who encourage and help in any way.

*Murray Bodo, O.F.M.*
*Susan Saint Sing*

# Foreword

We have both lived in Assisi and the Umbrian Valley.
We have both walked in the footsteps of Francis and
Clare. And we found in Assisi

a shadow of what
might be seen there if mind and heart

gave themselves to meditation,
deeper,

and deeper into Imagination's
holy forest, as travelers

followed the Zohar's dusty
shimmering roads, talking

with prophets and
hidden angels... [1]

Only, it was not the *Zohar*, but *The Little Flowers of St.
Francis'* dusty, shimmering roads we walked with other
pilgrims, through the places of Assisi talking with
prophets and hidden angels in secluded passageways
and cool shaded stones.

These places evoke images from the events that thrust
Francis and Clare into the role of helping revitalize the
Church following the reform Council of Lateran IV. Like
Calvary, like Bethlehem, which conjure up images of
Jesus and speak to our relationship with him, so, too, the
places of Francis and Clare. Perhaps more so than other

saints or spiritual writers the places of their lives seem to frame snapshots, give glimpses of the God/human, human/God intercourse.

As one man said when overlooking Assisi, standing above it at the castle on Mount Subasio with a warm summer breeze wafting in the late evening air—and fireflies dancing on the fragrant ginestra flowers—lights from the Umbrian plain stretching gray-hued into the purple-red twilight, "Anyone could be a saint here."

Of course, we know this statement is simplistic, but his insight is clear—there is a uniqueness to the place of Assisi and its environs. And this uniqueness of matter mingling with spirit will speak to your pilgrim heart if you look for and contemplate its reflections in your world.

Perhaps Nikos Kazantzakis captures this commingling best:

Toward the beginning of spring I arrived at Assisi, Italy's most sacred city. Gardens, rooftops, courtyards, the very air—all were filled with the invisible presence of God's sweet little pauper. It was Sunday. The massive bells of his church were ringing, and the shrill, silver-voiced bells of the convent of St. Clare were answering them from the small square opposite. The two of them, St. Clare and St. Francis: joined in the air, forever inseparable, with the immortal voices given them by sainthood and death. "Father Francis, when are you finally going to come and see us poor sisters in our convent?" "When the thorns blossom with white flowers... " And behold! thorns now blossom everlastingly, and God's two mated doves, forever inseparable, flap their wings eternally over Assisi.[2]

# Notes

[1] Denise Levertov, "A Letter to William Kintner of Muhlenberg," in *Poems: 1960-1967* (New York: New Directions, 1968).

[2] Nikos Kazantzakis, *Report to Greco* (New York: Simon and Schuster, 1965), p. 183.

# Introducing A Retreat With...

Twenty years ago I made a weekend retreat at a Franciscan house on the coast of New Hampshire. The retreat director's opening talk was as lively as a long-range weather forecast. He told us how completely God loves each one of us—without benefit of lively anecdotes or fresh insights.

As the friar rambled on, my inner critic kept up a sotto voce commentary: "I've heard all this before." "Wish he'd say something new that I could chew on." "That poor man really doesn't have much to say." Ever hungry for manna yet untasted, I devalued any experience of hearing the same old thing.

After a good night's sleep, I awoke feeling as peaceful as a traveler who has at last arrived safely home. I walked across the room toward the closet. On the way I passed the sink with its small framed mirror on the wall above. Something caught my eye like an unexpected presence. I turned, saw the reflection in the mirror and said aloud, "No wonder he loves me!"

This involuntary affirmation stunned me. What or whom had I seen in the mirror? When I looked again, it was "just me," an ordinary person with a lower-than-average reservoir of self-esteem. But I knew that in the initial vision I had seen God-in-me breaking through like a sudden sunrise.

At that moment I knew what it meant to be made in the divine image. I understood right down to my size eleven feet what it meant to be loved exactly as I was.

Only later did I connect this revelation with one granted to the Trappist monk-writer Thomas Merton. As he reports in *Conjectures of a Guilty Bystander*, while standing all unsuspecting on a street corner one day, he was overwhelmed by the "joy of being...a member of a race in which God Himself became incarnate.... There is no way of telling people that they are all walking around shining like the sun."

As an absentminded homemaker may leave a wedding ring on the kitchen windowsill, so I have often mislaid this precious conviction. But I have never forgotten that particular retreat. It persuaded me that the Spirit rushes in where it will. Not even a boring director or a judgmental retreatant can withstand the "violent wind" that "fills the entire house" where we dwell in expectation (see Acts 2:2).

So why deny ourselves any opportunity to come aside awhile and rest on holy ground? Why not withdraw from the daily web that keeps us muddled and wound? Wordsworth's complaint is ours as well: "The world is too much with us." There is no flu shot to protect us from infection by the skepticism of the media, the greed of commerce, the alienating influence of technology. We need retreats as the deer needs the running stream.

## An Invitation

This book and its companions in the *A Retreat With...* series from St. Anthony Messenger Press are designed to meet that need. They are an invitation to choose as director some of the most powerful, appealing and wise mentors our faith tradition has to offer.

Our directors come from many countries, historical eras and schools of spirituality. At times they are teamed to sing in close harmony (for example, Francis de Sales, Jane de Chantal and Aelred of Rievaulx on spiritual friendship). Others are paired to kindle an illuminating fire from the friction of their differing views (such as Augustine of Hippo and Mary Magdalene on human sexuality). All have been chosen because, in their humanness and their holiness, they can help us grow in self-knowledge, discernment of God's will and maturity in the Spirit.

Inviting us into relationship with these saints and holy ones are inspired authors from today's world, women and men whose creative gifts open our windows to the Spirit's flow. As a motto for the authors of our series, we have borrowed the advice of Dom Frederick Dunne to the young Thomas Merton. Upon joining the Trappist monks, Merton wanted to sacrifice his writing activities lest they interfere with his contemplative vocation. Dom Frederick wisely advised, "Keep on writing books that make people love the spiritual life."

That is our motto. Our purpose is to foster (or strengthen) friendships between readers and retreat directors—friendships that feed the soul with wisdom, past and present. Like the scribe "trained for the kingdom of heaven," each author brings forth from his or her storeroom "what is new and what is old" (Matthew 13:52).

## The Format

The pattern for each *A Retreat With...* remains the same; readers of one will be in familiar territory when they move on to the next. Each book is organized as a seven-session retreat that readers may adapt to their own schedules or to the needs of a group.

3

Day One begins with an anecdotal introduction called "Getting to Know Our Director(s)." Readers are given a telling glimpse of the guide(s) with whom they will be sharing the retreat experience. A second section, "Placing Our Director(s) in Context," will enable retreatants to see the guides in their own historical, geographical, cultural and spiritual settings.

Having made the human link between seeker and guide, the authors go on to "Introducing Our Retreat Theme." This section clarifies how the guide(s) are especially suited to explore the theme and how the retreatant's spirituality can be nourished by it.

After an original "Opening Prayer" to breathe life into the day's reflection, the author, speaking with and through the mentor(s), will begin to spin out the theme. While focusing on the guide(s)' own words and experience, the author may also draw on Scripture, tradition, literature, art, music, psychology or contemporary events to illuminate the path.

Each day's session is followed by reflection questions designed to challenge, affirm and guide the reader in integrating the theme into daily life. A "Closing Prayer" brings the session full circle and provides a spark of inspiration for the reader to harbor until the next session.

Days Two through Six begin with "Coming Together in the Spirit" and follow a format similar to Day One. Day Seven weaves the entire retreat together, encourages a continuation of the mentoring relationship and concludes with "Deepening Your Acquaintance," an envoi to live the theme by God's grace, the director(s)' guidance and the retreatant's discernment. A closing section of Resources serves as a larder from which readers may draw enriching books, videos, cassettes and films.

We hope readers will experience at least one of those memorable "No wonder God loves me!" moments. And we hope that they will have "talked back" to the mentor(s), as good friends are wont to do.

A case in point: There was once a famous preacher who always drew a capacity crowd to the cathedral. Whenever he spoke, an eccentric old woman sat in the front pew directly beneath the pulpit. She took every opportunity to mumble complaints and contradictions— just loud enough for the preacher to catch the drift that he was not as wonderful as he was reputed to be. Others seated down front glowered at the woman and tried to shush her. But she went right on needling the preacher to her heart's content.

When the old woman died, the congregation was astounded at the depth and sincerity of the preacher's grief. Asked why he was so bereft, he responded, "Now who will help me to grow?"

All of our mentors in *A Retreat With...* are worthy guides. Yet none would seek retreatants who simply said, "Where you lead, I will follow. You're the expert." In truth, our directors provide only half the retreat's content. Readers themselves will generate the other half.

As general editor for the retreat series, I pray that readers will, by their questions, comments, doubts and decision-making, fertilize the seeds our mentors have planted.

And may the Spirit of God rush in to give the growth.

*Gloria Hutchinson*
*Series Editor*
*Conversion of Saint Paul, 1995*

# Getting to Know Our Directors

When I think of Saint Francis and Saint Clare of Assisi, so many different images come to mind. I went to Assisi almost twenty years ago to be near Francis, his town, his mountains, for healing. I was a twenty-year-old looking for a way to make some sense of a year in which my father died, I suffered a severe neck and back injury, and I got divorced.

Having grown up in a mountain town in Pennsylvania, I was always close to Francis—or so I thought. Now, these twenty years later, on August 2, the Feast of the Portiuncula, his statue, a typical Saint Francis-With-the-Birds garden statue, lies face down in the dirt next to a hydrangea which it used to flank. I learned many things when I worked in Assisi to be close to him—I learned about Saint Clare, I learned about Don Aldo Brunacci, who risked his life during the Second World War to save Jews hiding in the Franciscan monasteries, I learned about the warmth of the Italian workers I shared my days with and who at night dealt me into a card game named *buon gioco* (explained to me in Italian and whose face values were not numerical) which I never caught on to and thus provided many laughs and good-natured jokes. I also learned that in Italian villages, when a saint is prayed to for a miracle, and that miracle does not happen, the women dig a hole in the ground in front of their house and turn the statue of the saint upside down in the hole until the prayer is answered. I do not have the strength to dig a hole so I laid the statue face down.

So I wait for my miracle. What do you wait for? What are you seeking from these two saints? Your reasons are your own, but perhaps this retreat will be a structure for you to climb.

I've been told that I should have prayed to Clare rather than Francis in the first place. Clare, a woman, gentle, a healer. Clare, a mystery of whom little is written, little is known, much is supposed. I used to sit all morning at the cafe across from the wall where Clare's childhood home stood in the Piazza San Rufino. I would stare at the wall, secretly hoping that a shutter would fling open and give me a glimpse of who Clare was. The piazza was usually speckled with darting bambinos kicking soccer balls. Teenagers tried desperately to ignore their younger brothers and sisters, an air of independence and importance in their stance.

Francis no doubt stood here with his group of friends. They too probably teased and laughed and conversed eloquently, trying to impress the townspeople with their newfound maturity and position. Years later he stood in another square alone, with no laughter, and laid his clothes at his father's feet, renouncing all his earthly possessions to follow his Father in heaven. Clare would have been only a little girl, maybe seven years old. But the scene left her with a deep, lasting impression and a longing to join this serious and mysterious young man.

Did Clare ever go back and visit her family after she ran away to join Francis? I know her sisters and even her mother came to live with her at San Damiano. But what about Clare's father? Did he approve, or was he in sympathy with Francis' father? How hard it must have been to live in peace of soul and mind with such unresolved disruptions in her family life.

Most of Clare's life can only be answered by more and more speculative questions. Who she really was and why is an unfinished puzzle. I have searched at her basilica and crypt, her cloister at San Damiano and at the site of her childhood home, hoping to find a continuous thread that will unravel her mysterious tapestry. But there is no single thread. There is only the braid of Clare's love—of God, of her sisters, of all people. And of course her love for Francis. Love? Certainly. Romantic love? Who knows? For one another? Certainly for Christ. It is the stuff of great literature juxtaposed on the fabric of their real lives whose threads weave rather austere pictures of war, imprisonment, suffering, sickness, poverty, the depths of which we most likely will never know, because these were medieval minds, medieval times of broadswords, lepers, dungeons.

Yet from this time of relative evolutionary poverty in world development and thought, a great spiritual phoenix rose from a tiny pink and white granite town slapped on the side of Mount Subasio in the Italian province of Umbria. It is my hope that a similar phoenix will stir in the concrete molded robes that lie in my garden. Will the sparrow entrusted to and cemented to Francis' statue ever fly?

So we search together through Francis and Clare's experiences to make some sense of our own experience, our own existence....

*Susan Saint Sing*


One summer evening, as I sat with two Assisi cab drivers drinking chamomile tea at the Bar Minerva in the Piazza del Comune, we heard the faint sounds of singing coming from above the city in the vicinity of the fortress called the Rocca Maggiore. As the strains grew louder, we recognized the melody: Donovan's "Brother Sun and Sister Moon," from the Franco Zeffirelli film of the same name. Soon we could see lights flickering in and out of the streets that wind down into the piazza. All eyes were now turned to the lane from which we expected these modern troubadours to emerge. Suddenly, the first pairs of a long procession of teenagers strode into the piazza, their hands holding candles, their voices raised in what seemed every European and English tongue. The whole piazza was flooded with light and joyful song, and one of the cab drivers, a tear caught in the corner of his eye, said, "I have to get home, away from all this sentimental stuff." The other cabbie winked knowingly at me as we watched our friend walk away, overcome with his own emotions.

This kind of thing happens over and again in Assisi. Pilgrimages of young people from all over the world coming to the town of Francis and Clare to find...what? God? Themselves? Meaning? Others searching like them for something to make sense of their lives, give purpose to their living, give a goal, a grail to pursue?

Perhaps it is hope that this is the end of the journey for their pilgrim hearts. Why else would they seek it here in this quiet, medieval town instead of going on to those two meccas of the art lover and the pilgrim, Florence to the north and Rome to the south? It is Francis, of course, and more and more it is Clare as well, who holds them in this little town. Francis and Clare of Assisi. Their very names are enough to make even the most callow youth or casual tourist pause and wonder about staying the night.

My own pilgrimage here began a long time ago when, as a boy of thirteen, I read a life of Saint Francis in a corner of the junior high library in Gallup, New Mexico. Twenty-two years later I stepped onto the train platform of Assisi, realizing that the journey to Assisi takes a long time because it is a journey of the soul.

Assisi for me is the town of symbols and mystery. It belongs somehow to the olive trees, and Francis and

Clare belong to them both. They are entertwined with the roots of these ancient trees and lie like mortar between the pink stones of Assisi's houses. In order to understand the radical and at times terrifying commitment of Francis and Clare to the crucified Christ, it is necessary to look at these old, twisted olive trees that cling tenaciously to the sides of Mount Subasio and that line the road from the city gate down to the monastery of San Damiano.

They are old; some say the oldest olive trees in Italy. They are rooted with a stubbornness akin to Francis' single-willed determination to follow the Christ who spoke to him from the crucifix of San Damiano, the crucifix which Clare peered into every day as into a mirror. Like these trees, Francis and Clare were immovable in their total devotion to gospel poverty—and like the olive trees, they have outlasted all the years and seasons of change and progress.

And like the pink stones of Assisi, Francis and Clare have remained attractive though architecture and styles in the Church have changed. The mortar of their spirits holds these stones together just as the real mortar Francis made with his own hands held together the first little churches he repaired: San Damiano, San Pietro, Santa Maria degli Angeli (which Francis called the Portiuncula, The Little Portion).

The outward configuration of trees changes, but they endure if they are rooted well. Franciscans, too, have changed in their configuration, but the roots are still there in the writings of Francis and Clare, in the spirit that breathes between their words, in the simple story of their lives, and in Assisi itself. There is more than mystique to this town. In the geography of Assisi is the landscape of Francis' and Clare's souls.

This retreat is a meditation on the spirituality of Francis and Clare from the viewpoint of the places in which it is rooted. Like the olive trees of Mount Subasio, Francis and Clare are inseparable from this land, this place and space of growing. Like the stones and mortar of its houses, they belong to this town. Always, they are Saint Francis and Saint Clare of *Assisi*. They invite us now to follow our pilgrim hearts, to make our gospel pilgrimage.

*Murray Bodo*

## Placing Our Directors in Context

### Francis

I, Francis, was born in 1182 to the wealthy Assisi cloth merchant, Pietro Bernardone, and my mother, the Lady Pica. And though the times were turbulent with pope and emperor warring for control of Italian city-states and a rising middle class vying with the nobility for power and influence, my youth was one of relative luxury, of gaiety and music. My consuming ambition was to be a knight like the legendary knight-errants of King Arthur's court.

And so, in my twentieth year I went to battle in a minor skirmish between Assisi and our neighbor city, Perugia. We were routed, and I was taken prisoner at Ponte San Giovanni, a small village between Assisi and Perugia. I spent a year in a Perugian prison and tried to make the best of a difficult situation, cheering my fellow prisoners and singing to keep my heart from despair.

Because I was wealthy, I was imprisoned with the nobles and other wealthy young men, not with the less fortunate citizens. This troubled me, as did my father's ransoming me on the grounds of illness when others had to remain in prison, though to be honest my health was breaking down. In fact, when I was released, I spent the year 1204 bedridden in my father's house—another kind of imprisonment.

When I finally rose from my bed, I walked the hills of Assisi, but they no longer lifted my heart. A light had gone out inside me. But even here God was with me, for in my darkness and desolation I began to hear the voices and see the visions that transformed my life and turned me into a child again.

The first voice came in a dream at Spoleto where I was bivouacked in another futile attempt to break out of my doldrums by going off to war as a knight. In the dream I saw the large room of a castle, its walls covered with shields which, a voice proclaimed, belonged to me and my followers. Waking, I was ready to embrace this prophecy of knighthood and glory, when I heard another voice:

"Francis, is it better to serve the Lord or the servant?"

"Oh, sir, the Lord, of course."

"Then why are you trying to turn your Lord into a servant?"

Suddenly I realized what Lord it was who spoke to me.

"Lord, what do you want me to do?"

"Return to Assisi. There it shall be revealed to you what you are to do, and you will come to understand the meaning of this vision."

And that is how and when I began to listen to God instead of my own impatient desire for glory on the battlefield. I began the long journey back to Assisi. Long because of the humiliation and shame I felt in seeming to be a coward shrinking from the fight, but short, too, because I knew at last that I was doing God's will and that made me run with joy.

Of course, turning from the battlefield was not as easy as it sounds, nor was it accomplished in the walk back from Spoleto. It cost me great pain and mental suffering. In fact, I spent the whole year after returning to Assisi trying to come to terms with what it would mean to do God's will.

Then, one day, as I was praying before the crucifix in the little, rundown chapel of San Damiano, the crucifix spoke: "Francis, go and repair my house which, as you see, is falling into ruin."

I took the Lord's words literally and set off to repair San Damiano. I snatched a bolt of cloth from my father's shop, mounted my horse, and rode off to the neighboring town of Foligno. There I sold the cloth and the horse and hiked back to the church of San Damiano. I offered the money to the astonished priest who recognized me and refused to accept the money. He rightly suspected that my prodigal giving was taking place without the knowledge or approval of my father. So I flung the money onto the windowsill and set out for Assisi to beg stones to repair God's church.

This was another turning point in my life because I realized that you repair God's house not with money but with stones acquired by overcoming shame and by begging.

Of course, no rich man's son can go around begging stones and dressing like a beggar without attracting attention—attention, and then ridicule and scorn. One day when I was begging and the crowd was mocking and catcalling after me, my father heard the noise and went to the door of his shop to see what was happening. To his dismay and shame he saw his own son being mocked through the streets.

Father was enraged at this new insult to the family honor. Only a few months before when I sold the cloth and horse, Father had dragged me home and locked me in one of the storage rooms. But when Father had to leave on a buying trip, Mother braved his wrath and released me. I went immediately to San Damiano to live there with the poor priest. And now this! It was too much for Father, and he rushed into the street and dragged me before Bishop Guido, demanding that I return the money for the cloth and horse.

Then—and I never know quite how to say this—I stripped off my clothes and there before the crowd gathered in the bishop's courtyard, I laid my clothes at Father's feet and uttered the most dramatic words of my young life:

"Listen to me, everybody! Up till now, I have called Pietro Bernardone my father! But now that I propose to serve God, I give him back not only his money, but all the clothes I have from him. From now on, I can advance naked before the Lord, saying in truth no longer, 'My father, Pietro Bernardone, but, Our Father who art in heaven.'"

Don't ask me how I managed to get these words out, for all I can say is that from that moment on I began in earnest to live the gospel literally. And thus began the journey from the house of Pietro Bernardone to the house of God.

Soon others began to follow in my footsteps, the first of whom was a wealthy merchant of Assisi named Bernard of Quintavalle.

He invited me to his home one day, and after the evening meal, we retired for the night. Soon Bernard began to snore deeply, and I knew it was safe to rise from the bed and pray. As I prayed over and over all night long, "My God and my all," Bernard, I learned the next morning, was listening, only pretending to be asleep. He asked me then what he should do to become God's servant.

I answered that we should go to Mass at the church of

Saint Nicholas and after Mass ask the priest to open the book of the Gospels for us three times. Which we did, and this is where the pages fell:

> "If you wish to be perfect, go and sell all your possessions, and give to the poor...and come, follow me."
> "Take nothing for your journey, neither staff nor knapsack, shoes nor money."
> "If any will come after me, let them renounce self, take up their cross and follow me."

And that is what Bernard did, beginning a movement that would flower into three orders: the Order of Friars Minor, the Order of the Poor Ladies, and the Order of Lay People living the gospel in the world.

Our story is too long to record here, so let me simply say that we flourished in gospel living, begging alms and ministering with the lepers.

God put the final seal to our way of life on a mountain called La Verna. I went there in early September, 1224, in order to prepare for the feast of Saint Michael the Archangel. There I prayed, "O Lord, I beg of you two graces before I die—to experience in myself in all possible fullness the pains of your cruel Passion, and to feel for you the same love that made you sacrifice yourself for us."

God's "Yes" was an embrace so complete that my side and hands and feet were sealed with the wounds of Christ's love, the marks of his holy Passion.

In the final two years after receiving the stigmata, I continued to preach and witness as a herald of the Great King. And when I died on October 3, 1226, they say there was seen a light over Mount Subasio, a light that you, pilgrim heart, may still feel filtering down the slopes of the mountain and through the streets and lanes of Assisi. All I can leave you with is that light and these words, "I have done what was mine to do; may Christ teach you what you are to do."

## Clare

Clare. Clara. Chiara. My name, they say, like my life, is full of the clarity of light. A light that shone in Assisi and throughout the Umbrian countryside for sixty years. A light that continued shining for twenty-seven years after Francis' death, as a bright illumination of Holy Poverty. In some ways I was the Lady Poverty for the early brothers and for the Poor Ladies of San Damiano. Not that I boast of this. On the contrary, if I was such a light, such an image of the Lady Poverty, it was because of the sweet embrace of the Poor Crucified Christ, who reached down from his holy cross to lift me, his poor creature, into his arms.

I was born in Assisi in 1193. My family was a knightly one, and therefore my early life was one of privilege and wealth. My father, Favarone, was a knight of the house of Offreduccio, and my mother, Ortolana, was in her own right an extraordinary woman. She made the three pilgrimages to Rome, Jerusalem and Monte Gargano, the shrine of Saint Michael the Archangel—an extraordinary feat, given the dangers and hardships involved in leaving the protection of one's own walled city. After father's death, mother joined us at San Damiano, as had my sister Agnes and Beatrice before her. But I am getting ahead of my story.

Even as a child I loved to pray and give alms. I felt deeply the pain of the poor, especially the lepers. And when my father offered me the hand of a suitor, I refused, not because I had another earthly lover, but because Christ himself had become my lover. Holding close this secret, I continued to search my heart for discernment. How was I to respond fully to the love of Jesus Christ, who had stolen my heart?

And then Francis entered my life. I began to hear stories of the rich son of Pietro Bernardone who had renounced his father's riches and who walked Assisi's streets dressed like a beggar, and in fact, begging, though he was the son of one of the richest men in Assisi. It was rumored, too, that he had taken up residence with the lepers who lived on the plain below the town near the church of St. Mary of the Angels.

At last I had found a kindred soul, someone who was doing precisely what my own heart kept moving me to do: to follow in the footsteps of the Poor Christ. And so, accompanied by my friend, Bona, I arranged clandestine meetings with Francis. From those encounters came the jelling of my vocation. I would join Francis and his brothers, and my friend Pacifica was determined to go with me.

Bishop Guido, who was privy to my meetings with Francis, signalled the time of our investiture. On Palm Sunday, March 17, 1212, instead of waiting at the altar for me to come and receive the palm, Bishop Guido descended the altar steps and handed me the palm where I stood. This proferred palm became my engagement ring signalling the time of my betrothal to Christ.

That very night Pacifica and I fled from Father's palazzo next to the Cathedral of San Rufino and walked out the city gates, down the hillside, through the poppy and wheat fields with their promise of spring shimmering in the moonlight, and entered the church of St. Mary of the Angels.

Francis and the brothers were waiting, lit candles in their hands. Francis himself cut our hair and clothed us in the rough habit of poverty and encircled our young waists with the cord of chastity and obedience to Christ.

After the ceremony of investiture, Francis and the brothers accompanied us to San Paolo, a Benedictine convent of nuns near Bastia. We remained there only a few days before joining a community of religious women at Sant' Angelo di Panzo on the side of Mount Subasio, where we were joined by my younger sister Catherine (whom Francis later named Agnes). This decision was one too many for our family, and Uncle Monaldo, the feudal chief, was dispatched to bring Agnes home, by force if necessary.

When Monaldo and his knights arrived and began to drag Agnes away, I fell to my knees and prayed until Agnes grew heavy in the knights' hands—so heavy that they could no longer lift her or even drag her. No amount of effort availed, and they were forced to leave the leaden Agnes where they dropped her. How great is the power of prayer!

Shortly afterwards, Bishop Guido offered us the church of San Damiano where I remained for the rest of my life. Agnes was later made Abbess of Monticelli near Florence but returned to San Damiano toward the end of my life, and Pacifica went to a newly-founded monastery in Spello for one year.

San Damiano was the first church Francis restored after hearing Christ's words, "Francis, go and repair my house which, as you see, is falling into ruin." And as Francis was restoring this house, he prophesied truly that some day it would be the home of holy virgins betrothed to Christ.

From the moment I entered San Damiano, I knew I was home. Here was where I would live out the dream of my childhood—to be the bride of Christ in Christ's own home. Here we democratized the previously hierarchical life of the monastery. All the sisters were equal, no matter what their station in the world. Here with my sisters, I wrote a Rule of Life, the first Rule written by women and approved by the Church. Here we lived the hidden life of contemplatives, a life of prayer and silence and humble service to one another.

But though we were servants, we were also ladies of the castle, as in the tales of chivalry and courtly love. The troubadours I heard in Father's palazzo sang of the ideal woman, the lady of the castle, whom the true knight was able to woo from the castle's lord by daring deeds, by chivalrous conduct, by courtesy, the virtue of the knight.

One troubadour, Jaufre Rudel, began to sing of a woman he had never seen and to extol the greater virtue of *amor de lonh*, love from afar. This idealized woman became the Lady Poverty for Francis, and we became for him incarnations of Lady Poverty, the brides of Christ.

There is an incident in my life and that of the Poor Ladies that shows our knightly character, as well. When the mercenary soldiers of the Emperor Frederick II were poised outside the city of Assisi ready to begin their seige by first seizing the monastery of San Damiano, I had the Blessed Sacrament brought to the opened door of the dormitory. And when the mercenary soldiers beheld the Eucharistic Christ, they retreated, and Assisi was spared. It was September, 1240, when we, like Francis and the brothers, acted like knights and repelled the attackers of our city.

Through all the years, we tried to hold true to Francis' gospel ideal of poverty by living without fixed incomes or dowries, a privilege granted us by Pope Innocent III in 1216 and renewed by Pope Gregory IX in 1228. Then on my deathbed, the day before I died, August 11, 1253, I received papal approval of our Rule of Life.

To the glory of God. Amen.

# Day One
## Going Forth, Going Within

### Introducing Our Retreat Theme

Francis' life was lived on the road, and Clare's in the monastery of San Damiano. These are the two dimensions of Franciscan spirituality, pilgrimage and retreat, the going forth and the going within, each complementing and facilitating the other.

The monastery of San Damiano. Here Francis heard the voice from the crucifix saying to him, "Francis, go and rebuild my house which, as you see, is falling into ruin."

Francis heard that voice and began immediately to beg stones to repair the crumbling church of San Damiano, prophesying as he worked that this church would one day be the dwelling place of the Poor Ladies. And so it was. Clare and her Poor Ladies took up residence there, and it became the Castle of Lady Poverty, just as the road became the apostolic journey for Francis and his brothers.

Our retreat will focus on both: the road and the retreat. The road becomes a journey into the monastery of San Damiano, our retreat from labor on the road. We retreat in order to return refreshed to the road, to the basilicas and piazzas to proclaim the Good News by the example of our lives, a proclaiming that tires us, drains us so that we later return to San Damiano, retreat there into the depths of the soul. Pilgrimage and retreat. The poles of our life in Christ, the two complementarities, Francis and Clare of Assisi. Clare is retreat; Francis is pilgrimage. There is no retreat without pilgrimage, no pilgrimage without retreat.

Your retreat might be as close as your backyard swing or a parish retreat house in the nearby countryside. Our text and our descriptions serve only as guides; as Francis' and Clare's friendship guides us through our daily lives, their places and the events which occurred there become images in our lives where we seek similar peace, conversion and renewal.

A windowsill with a geranium in your house could be Saint Clare's garden if the light it catches or the petal it opens brings you the solace which that medieval garden brought to them.


## Opening Prayer

Loving God, open my heart and my imagination to make this journey with Francis and Clare. As I walk the streets of Assisi in my mind, make my inner journey this day a walk with you, as Saint Francis and Saint Clare walked in faith with you. May this inner journey help me to walk through my day more slowly, noticing that my own home, the streets of my neighborhood, are no less than the Assisi of Francis and Clare. For this is where I live, where I, too, can grow in holiness as Francis and Clare grew in holiness where they lived.

# RETREAT SESSION ONE

It may seem strange that we are here conjoining pilgrimage with retreat, but this marriage of the outer and inner journey has been the pattern of both retreatants and pilgrims for centuries. Medieval pilgrims, for example, believed that when they went on pilgrimage to Jerusalem, they were making four simultaneous pilgrimages: the literal, outer journey to Jerusalem; an allegorical or symbolic journey to the roots of the Church; a tropological or figurative journey into the soul; and an anagogical or mystical journey to the heavenly Jerusalem. This is the dynamic Dante uses in the *Divine Comedy*, a dynamic that was more than a textual one. It was what medieval pilgrims actually experienced, or hoped to experience when they went on pilgrimage.

The medieval dynamic is the modern, as well. A pilgrimage is a retreat into the soul, as well as an outer journey.

We will try to illustrate this dynamic as concretely as possible. We will concentrate our visit on the plain below Assisi, the basilicas of Clare and Francis, San Damiano and the Portiuncula. Though there are many more places significant to Francis' life in particular, we have chosen these places for their importance to both Francis and Clare. The road is circuitous, with cutbacks in the hills, decisions, backtracking. The wonder of the mystery unfolding begins at the train station itself, for the Assisi train station is not Assisi. It is "Santa Maria degli Angeli," St. Mary of the Angels, the "new" city below medieval Assisi, which you can see as you emerge from the ocher-colored, stuccoed depot, a walled city floating in summer haze like a vision of Camelot on a spur of Mount Subasio that towers over the whole valley of Spoleto. Or is it winter? spring? fall?

And so you arrive on the plain below Assisi, where Saint Francis, like Christ, gathered the five thousand— friars all—for a Chapter of Mats, to be fed by Christ's word, Christ's Body—gathered them like those after Christ's Resurrection, again in numbers something like five thousand—believers all—to hear Peter, as the friars came to hear Francis, as now you've come to listen to his voice here on the plain before you ascend the holy mountain, Subasio, to Assisi.

St. Mary of the Angels, the "Portiuncula," the hearth of the Order of St. Francis, which the early Friars rented from the Benedictine monks of Mount Subasio for a basket of fish—Jesus, by the sea of Tiberias, with some fish cooking over a charcoal fire. You have begun the mythic journey forward to Assisi, backward and inward to the shore of the Tiberian Sea, where Jesus shows himself to the disciples after rising from the dead.

You are on the train platform, having just disembarked. If you have come from Rome via Foligno, where you may have changed trains—and where Saint Francis exchanged his father's horse for coins for the lamp of the chapel of San Damiano, whose crucifix had just spoken to him. If you've come that way, then when you watch your train depart for Perugia—where Francis as a young man lingered a year in prison—as the last train car speeds by, suddenly ahead and to your left looms the massive Basilica of St. Mary of the Angels, which holds under its central dome the Portiuncula, the "Little Portion," the chapel which Francis restored with his own hands. There, as to the tomb of Christ, he bade Pope Innocent III to send pilgrims for a plenary indulgence in lieu of going on crusade to the Holy Land, or making the long, expensive journey perilous to Rome and the tomb of the Apostle Peter.

Here then, you stand suitcase in hand. Your suitcase may literally be filled with clothes, or perhaps it is filled with memories, hurt, happiness. Perhaps it is empty, waiting to be filled; perhaps you bring your family, or a need.

The Portiuncula is the womb of Saint Francis' charism and of his order dedicated to Our Lady, Mary of the Angels. Here Francis died on October 3, 1226, and here he gave the Church the first nonviolent option for a plenary indulgence—a pilgrimage to the woman, Mary, instead of the phallic thrust of spear and sword toward Jerusalem. And how important that option is, and was, for a people besieged and sacked, beset by bitter internecine struggles over and again into the sixteenth century.

Have you come to accumulate? What? Experience? Grace? Merit? You will find none of that here. For here is a place of no accumulation, no appropriation. *Appropriatio*, Saint Francis named it—that taking, claiming, for oneself what belongs to the Great Almsgiver, the Most High God, *Altissimu, Omnipotente, Bon Signore*. The Good Lord, who lends us everything for our liberal use, but not for *appropriatio*, for accumulating where moth and rust consume.

And so you, pilgrim, leave behind, relinquish what you have seen, what you have experienced. You move on. You walk from the train platform through the plastic-beaded curtain that reminds you of the movie *Casablanca*, into the station bar. You leave this view of Santa Maria degli Angeli to whoever is next to stand on the platform watching the last train car speed by and discovering the great dome is so near.

Cappuccino. Capuchin. Coffee and Franciscan, the coffee so called because of the cowl-like color of its bearded foam. This cappuccino may be the first "Franciscan" you encounter before emerging into the

25

train station's sunlit piazza where you suddenly see—
beyond the buses and taxis, the luggage and bustling,
waiting passengers—Assisi. Two miles or so away, it
waits for you. You do not try a cappuccino—as you will
not try other things along the way—not dare to order
when you know no Italian, when you are anxious,
desperate perhaps, not to miss your bus or taxi to the old
city of Saint Francis. Who, after all, could stop and try a
cappuccino now when who knows when another train
will stop, another bus be waiting? And so you walk
through the bar and out into the piazza.

But before you leave, look. See this station. You will
see many more. They are more than places of entry and
departure. They are texts. They are Italo Calvino writing:

> In the odor of the station there is a passing whiff of
> station cafe odor. There is someone looking through
> the befogged glass, he opens the glass door of the
> bar, everything is misty, inside, too, as if seen by
> nearsighted eyes, or eyes irritated by coal dust. The
> pages of the book are clouded like the windows of
> an old train, the cloud of smoke rests on the
> sentences....
>
> Stations are all alike; it doesn't matter if the
> lights cannot illuminate beyond their blurred halo,
> all of this is a setting you know by heart, with the
> odor of train that lingers even after all the trains
> have left, the special odor of stations after the last
> train has left. The lights of the station and the
> sentences you are reading seem to have the job of
> dissolving more than of indicating the things that
> surface from a veil of darkness and fog.[1]

Just as Calvino's novel begins in the smoke and fog and
anonymity of that as-yet-undefined railway station, so
you stand in this station which will become all the

stations—stations of the cross? of resurrection?—of your pilgrimage. All is as yet undefined, unacquired, unacquirable, like this moment in the train station—of Santa Maria degli Angeli? or Assisi?—which is yours only in imagination. It is yours only in what you can take with you, even without a souvenir—as you walk out into the sunlit? darkened? foggy? rainy? piazza of buses and taxis. All is as yet vague like the obscure medieval city people point to, looking as distant as the postcards others have sent you—taken, it seems, from this very spot where you stand, having not yet entered the city or even traveled the seven, almost eight, centuries to its arched gates.

## For Reflection

- *As I set out to follow my pilgrim heart, how do I hope Francis and Clare will make their presence known to me? Why have I chosen these two saints of Assisi as my mentors?*

- *In what particular ways might this pilgrimage-retreat enable me to grow in holiness? As I consider Saint Francis' teaching on* appropriatio, *what feelings, attitudes or memories are aroused in me? How might I respond to this teaching?*

- *How have stations of any kind marked my life as a pilgrim? Who are the most memorable pilgrims I have met in the stations and along the roads of my faith journey? How have they influenced or changed me?*

## Closing Prayer

Lord, though we walk abroad, let our manner
nevertheless be as humble and decorous as if we were in
a hermitage or a cell. For, as Saint Francis counsels us,
wherever we are and go, we have our cell with us.
Brother Body is our cell, and our soul is the hermit living
indoors in the cell, in order to pray to God and meditate
on God. If our soul does not remain in retirement in its
cell, then a hand-built cell is of little use.

St. Francis, help us to carry our cell with us always,
and may the Blessed Trinity dwell there forever. Amen.

### Notes

[1] Italo Calvino, *If on a winter's night a traveler* (Orlando, Fla.:
Harcourt Brace Jovanovich, 1979), p. 10.

# Day Two
## The Leper Hospital

### Coming Together in the Spirit

*In the Middle Ages many towns had a leper hospital. Midway between Assisi and the Portiuncula the present-day Casa Gualdi stands on the site of the thirteenth-century San Salvatore delle Pareti leper hospital. According to early Franciscan sources, one day on the road Francis overcame himself and embraced a leper, and the stench of the leper's sores were transformed into sweetness at this beginning of Francis' inner conversion to God.*

You have probably never seen a leper, let alone hundreds of these people in a leper colony. But this modern stuccoed villa with healthy green plants and shaded grasses was the once-dilapidated leper hospital where Francis and his brothers came daily to minister.

Today the road is well-traveled and attractive. But in Francis' day, though it was a branch of the main thoroughfare from Rome to France, it passed through forest and marshland suitable only, it was thought, for lepers, criminals and other social outcasts. You wonder how often Francis heard the blood-chilling warning, "Unclean! Unclean!" And how often did he wince or run or hold his breath and turn his eyes away as an infected leper was led past him and his friends beyond the town walls into the wilds? Little did he know that one day he would choose to join them and learn from them the paradox of redemption.

What did he see in that first leper's eyes that drew him close? What did he recognize that drove him to embrace this "foul and repugnant" being? Perhaps he saw his own soul as he himself envisioned it: rotting, stinking, slowly being eaten away by an undesired, invisible evil, yet with a deep underlying stream of goodness, integrity and compassion. He saw and accepted the lepers' ugliness and deformity, but he also saw them as human beings, people created and loved by God. They stirred in his heart a memory of his own illness and rejection and released a great longing to help.

Francis considered himself the greatest sinner God could find. What better instrument to reveal God's redeeming power and healing love? So too with the lepers; their "uncleanness" became a living symbol of his own sinfulness. Here among their mats and bandages he would accept both the light and the darkness present in all human existence. Francis was slowly healed by the gratitude of the lepers as he mercifully washed away their loneliness and tended their sores. And the lepers breathed new life fresh with the Spirit of God and fragrant in the knowledge that they were purposeful and useful, able to give life in return for the comfort and concern given to them.

Francis used this place as a training ground for those who would follow him. They too must recognize their true selves and accept their inner darkness, lest they be forever deceived into believing that because they had given their lives to God they were incapable of evil.

How wise you really were, Francis, to know that there is a leper in all of us that must be brought into the healing presence of God, to be tended to before we are transformed into life.

### Defining Our Thematic Context

Who is it we pass by in our headlong pursuit of God?
Francis learned to notice what lay or huddled by the
roadside. Often, the detour in life, that which seems to
slow you down or get you off the track, is really the way,
or if not the way, then at least a lesson in how to find the
way to God. We find the way by listening to Jesus at
home in our pilgrim hearts.

### Opening Prayer

When you see a poor person, you are looking at a
mirror of the Lord and his poor mother. So, too, in the
sick you are contemplating the kind of infirmities he took
upon himself for us.—Saint Francis

# RETREAT SESSION TWO

Already here, outside the train station, the spirit of the
"Poverello" and of the Lady Poverty, Clare, is shadowing
you and you will take a bus instead of the more expensive
taxi—at least you will consider doing so. You will ride
with others of all walks and persuasions, of different
countries and ethnic heritages. Together you will ascend
the holy hill to Assisi, sitting, standing, perhaps jostled
and cramped and pinched. You are on a real pilgrimage
with real people—no longer the fantasy of what you

imagined it to be.

And as you turn out of the station piazza and travel to the end of the short street, the view of Assisi is blocked by the apartments that line the road to the corner where you will turn right and begin bouncing toward the eastern end of Assisi where you will see very shortly the fortress-like foundations of the Basilica of St. Francis. Because you are all intent, as are all of your companions, on reaching the monumental city beyond, with its pink stones, its great basilicas of Saint Francis and Saint Clare, its medieval streets that you imagine Francis walked; because you are all intent on what lies ahead, you fail to see what has fallen by the roadside, what lies just off the road to your left about a kilometer from the train station. Even today it is called *Casa Gualdi, L'ospizio*, the hospice, the former leprosarium of San Salvatore delle Pareti, which at the time of Saint Francis was served by the Crosier Hospitaller Canons. Francis served in this place and he taught his brothers to serve in this place.

At the end of his life, when Francis is dying, his litter borne on the shoulders of his friars, he asks them to stop on his journey from the bishop's palace in Assisi to his beloved Portiuncula, on the plain below the city. Here he raises himself a bit and blesses his city for the last time from this spot where his vocation began, where he lived with and served the lepers, a ministry and way of life so central to Saint Francis' very being, that he begins his *Last Testament* with these words:

* Testament with these words:

> This is the way the Lord granted me, Brother
> Francis, to begin to do penance. When I was in sins,
> it seemed too bitter a thing even to look at lepers,
> and then the Lord himself led me among them, and
> I worked mercy together with them. And when I left
> them, that which had before seemed bitter was now

changed for me into sweetness of soul and body.[1]

No monument here. No shrine. No indication of its centrality in Francis' life, except for a bas-relief of Francis blessing the city, a bas-relief donated by the Franciscan scholar, Paul Sabatier, in 1910.

Sabatier understood. The journey with Francis begins on the plain *below* Assisi with those people and things we dismiss in the headlong pursuit of the stone monuments and churches above. What falls by the roadside is of infinitely more value to the Franciscan than what travels easily to and fro, or what lies at the end of the journey for those whose way is smooth and flat. This marginal spot, gives a perspective that allows one to "see" Assisi, as Jerusalem is seen for what it is, from outside the original city, where Jesus wept over it, where he died on Golgotha outside the city walls. So would Francis see Assisi from outside its walls, as would Clare from San Damiano outside the walls of Assisi. As they were conformed to Jesus' life, so would they be conformed to their Savior's dying, as well, outside the walls.

What is it, then, Francis said as he blessed his city here, or "there" now, since you have sped by Casa Gualdi before you even noticed it, not having prepared for that more important journey beyond tours and junkets?

Lord, it is believed that in olden days this city was a refuge of evil people. But now it is clear that in your large mercy and at a time of your choosing, you have shown your special superabundant compassion. Through your goodness alone, you have chosen Assisi to be a place of refuge for those who know you in truth, who give glory to your holy name, and who waft toward all Christians the perfume of right reputation, holy life, true doctrine, and evangelical perfection. Therefore I pray you, O

Lord Jesus Christ, father of mercies, do not dwell on
our ingratitude, but remember always the immense
compassion you have shown this city. Let it always
be a place of refuge for those who really know you
and glorify your blessed name forever. Amen.

A place of refuge throughout the ages. A leprosarium
outside its walls in the Middle Ages. A hospital city for
the Germans in World War II—and ironically, a hiding
place for Jews at the same time. Such is the mystery of
God and Assisi, then and now.

They rise in the mind, those who gave refuge in this
place to Jews escaping the Nazis; they rise like the carob
trees planted in their honor on Jerusalem's Avenue of the
Righteous Gentiles: Padre Rufino Niccacci, Bishop
Nicolini, Don Aldo Brunacci. And those others who in
1955 received gold medals from the Jewish community of
Italy: Padre Todde, Mother Giuseppina and the printer,
Luigi Brizi. Names revered by the Jewish refugees they
robed as friars and nuns and harbored in Assisi
monasteries and convents, in parishoners' homes. With
fake identity cards printed by Luigi Brizi they found jobs
and became a part of the commune of Assisi during the
war. All under the good, probably knowing eye of
Colonel Valentin Muller, the German Commandant of
Assisi. You will see his monument as you begin your
ascent from the first stop at the Basilica of St. Francis to
the Basilica of St. Clare.

You are now beginning to see the wonders along the
road.

As you begin the ascent to Saint Francis' Basilica, the
Valley of Spoleto will begin to reveal itself in all its light
expanse. It runs for thirty miles from Perugia in the
north, through Assisi and Foligno, to Spoleto in the
south. Its width, you may surmise as you look out the

window of the bus, is about five miles. The mountain in front of you is Mount Subasio, which rises to a height of four thousand nine hundred feet. You are in the Province of Umbria along the western slopes of the Apennine Mountains, about halfway between Florence and Rome.

Midway between Florence and Rome, midway between art and religion, the prince and the pope. A symbolic center. Midway, too, the *road* between. *Nel mezzo del cammin di nostra vita,* Dante phrases it. "In the middle of our life's way." Midpoint, then. A point of consciousness looking before and after. A point of decision, whether to proceed as before carrying everything we have brought with us so far, or to discard and surrender to what leads *us,* what we no longer try in vain to control. Depending, of course, on where we find ourselves. Is it the *selva selvaggia, oscura* of Dante, that "dark wood and wild"? Is it not always that Dantesque forest for pilgrims, no matter where we are when we begin to awaken to the reality that we are midway in life's journey?

In the middle of the way. Will it be here in Assisi that your awakening occurs, that awareness of being in a "wild forest" which fills you with fear and which you "know" you will never escape from unless someone leads you, your own Virgil, your own Beatrice? Are you midway through your life? through a divorce? through pregnancy? Be led.

Francis. Clare. Like Virgil and Beatrice for Dante, they will lead you through the hell of awakening, up the seven-story mountain of purgatory's cleansing, to vision's surrender, which is Paradise. That vision which elicits surrender to God's will. The "in his will is our peace" of Dante, *E'n la sua volontade e nostra pace.*

But we are ahead of the journey, as we so often are. We have to wait for the body, the physical, to catch up, to journey with us. To leave the body behind and get ahead of ourselves is the first great temptation of the pilgrim— to substitute the intellectual, the knowing, for the doing: I know what the journey is, therefore I do not have to make it.

Pilgrimage is first of all a physical journey. *Peregrinum.* Latin. One who comes from foreign parts, a stranger. Therefore, one who feels dis-located, out of place, whose mind, in traveling forward, wants to diminish, erase that strangeness the body experiences here in a foreign land, but cannot succeed by any thinking or even by charms and incantations. The body must go along, whether you are leper, refugee, soldier, hero, saint, philosopher, pilgrim.

You are still climbing, the bus doing your work for you. Though you have not yet begun to do your own climbing, you have at least surrendered to the journey itself. And as you ascend, you think of Saint Francis barefoot, or sandaled, walking up and down the Umbrian hills: you think of Clare barefoot on the cold floors of San Damiano, walking to and from her sisters, whose feet she washes in healing, nourishing love. Everything was slower then because it took longer to arrive; yet when one did arrive, body and soul were there together, and not, as in the modern world where the body, because of rapid, indeed, supersonic transportation, arrives before you have arrived psychologically.

Perhaps you are still at home, having not departed emotionally, mentally, though your body is here. This then is the second obstacle: traveling too fast, so that you are physically ahead of where you are emotionally, not having taken the time for parting and journeying and arriving. We cannot leave the body behind in the ascent to God, but neither can we ascend the real mountains, cross real oceans and land masses, without allowing the soul its grievings in saying good-bye, its fear of crossings, its wanting to return (*come pellegrin che tornar vuole*, "like a pilgrim who wants to return," *Purgatorio*, I, 49), its chances to greet the new.

Here, then, is where all the tensions and conflicts, the turning points, and integration begin: in the dichotomy (itself a false splitting of the person) between body and soul—a dichotomy which reveals itself (1) in overintellectualizing and fantasizing that precludes action, or/and (2) in precipitous action which leaves reflection and feeling behind; and it all begins to reveal itself here as you ascend to Assisi.

## For Reflection

- *In what ways (if any) have I felt like a social outcast, a marginal person, one huddled by the roadside unnoticed by others? Who has been my Francis in times like these?*

- *In what ways have I ministered to lepers of one kind or another? What parallels can I draw between them and me? How have I overcome (or how do I need to overcome) any feelings of repulsion toward the lepers of my world?*

- *Is there something repulsive in my life that I need to embrace? What is it? Who or what can help me to own this aspect of myself?*

- *What do I look forward to, remember or experience right now about the middle of my life's journey? How might the stories of fellow pilgrims (in life, in Scripture, in literature) help me to act wisely and well as my pilgrimage continues?*

## Closing Prayer

You each must know your own physical makeup
and allow your body its needs, so that it has
strength to serve the spirit. For just as we are bound
to avoid overindulgence in food, which harms both
body and soul, we must also avoid exaggerated
abstinence.—Saint Francis, *Mirror of Perfection*, 27

# DAY THREE
## San Damiano

### Coming Together in the Spirit

This is the church which Francis restored in 1205 when the crucifix miraculously spoke to him. It was the first cloister of the Poor Clares and where Francis came in his illness to be cared for by Clare. Here he wrote the "Canticle of Brother Sun." At his death his body was passed through the small window in the apse to be reverenced by Clare and her sisters one final time. Clare died here in 1253. Her body was later removed to her basilica and a new cloister built in her honor within Assisi's walls. Today San Damiano is occupied by the friars and remains much as it was in the time of Francis and Clare.

In the darkness of the last pew you can touch the damp stones and murmur, "Brother Rock." Here, cradled by their strength and shelter Francis becomes present to you; you understand what Jesus meant when he said "...the very stones would cry out" (Luke 19:40). The cross that spoke to Francis is not here anymore. It was given to the Poor Clares, and it hangs today at the Basilica of St. Clare.

It was at his Baptism, amidst all the splendor and wealth of the Cathedral of San Rufino, that Francis received the Holy Spirit, but it was here in this poor, crumbling, forgotten ruin that he met God.

The church was probably quiet that day, as it is today. Unabashed, Francis slips down to the side of the altar and sits staring at the heaps of rubble and dust. He has been here before; he wonders why he has come again. Moments pass into hours, but still he sits, legs falling asleep beneath him. He has nowhere else to go but here. This is his home, he belongs here for some unknown reason.

Perhaps it is the solitude. With no one watching his comings and goings he can talk aloud or shout his questions and raise his fist in anger at his confusion and lack of direction. He can also sink down with tears burning his eyes and sob, "Who are you, Lord? Why do you draw me in, as if on a baited line? What could you want of me? I am no one, I don't even particularly care for your ceremony and tithes...yet, I love you."

The dam breaks and he stands before the crucifix trying to grasp the suspended wood to feel some comfort, some empathy from the painted, linear wounds. His tears reveal the gilded cross beneath its dust, but still it hangs lifeless and dumb. He pushes away, ready to leave, angrily thinking that he has cried out futilely again.

"Francis."

He stops frozen in his steps.

"Francis!" It is louder.

He knows that voice. He has heard it before in his dreams, at Spoleto. He turns and faces the cross, which now has pulse and depth. Life surges around him as the world echoes his name.

"Go and repair my house, which as you see, is falling to ruin around you."

He listens for more. It seems the universe held its breath for a moment, but now the voice is gone. He hears only the wind in the olive trees. The cross hangs lifeless again. He falls to his knees, weeping tears of joy and ecstasy. "Yes, my Lord." At last a sign! Direction and purpose! Not immediately recognizing the breadth of the command, Francis sets off to find rocks and mortar to rebuild San Damiano's walls.

Whatever he received in that sacred encounter was the precious impetus to holiness that has been given to so few, yet sought by so many. And as you walk back up the dusty road to Assisi, you can see Francis, running and leaping half crazed, grabbing people's shoulders and twirling them around in a make-believe minuet of love. Love—that is what Francis met in San Damiano. And that is why he was able to skip lightly in glee rather than walk somberly away from such a weighty command.

## Defining Our Thematic Context

The small church of San Damiano outside the walls of Assisi is special to both Francis and Clare. It is the church Francis restored with his own hands, the church whose crucifix spoke to Francis. But San Damiano is more. San Damiano's is a dual charism that leads us into the heart of both Francis and Clare.

## Opening Prayer

Saint Francis writes to Clare and her sisters,
"Because by means of Divine inspiration you have made yourselves daughters and servants of the most high sovereign King, our Father in Heaven, and have espoused yourselves to the Holy Spirit in choosing to live according to the perfection of the Holy Gospel, I propose and promise that personally

and through my brothers I will always give you the same attentive care and special concern as to them."—from the *Rule of the Poor Clares*

Brother Francis, help us to care for one another as you and your brothers did for Clare and her sisters. We see your care even today in Franciscan churches, schools, hospitals. Help us to personally feel your presence and move our human hearts through your intercession to live and share the love and care of the holy gospel with our families, friends, neighbors, strangers.

# RETREAT SESSION THREE

You are just about to the top of the bus run, just about, not midway as in Dante's ride, but almost to the top. The bus will go on but you disembark at the parking lot below the final turn into the city, the parking lot for tourist buses. There is an escalator there to lift you up to one gate of the city, the Porta Nuova. But you do not ascend yet. You descend down a dirt road lined with olive trees to the small chapel of San Damiano where Francis' pilgrimage journey began.

As you step into the small courtyard at the side of the church, geraniums burst forth from their clay pots around the courtyard well, and the eaves and the overhangs of the outside walkway are dotted with swallows' nests. This was Clare's and the Poor Ladies' courtyard. From here they could see Mount Subasio though they did not walk its paths. The journeys Clare and her sisters made were in their heart. They could be in heaven with their Lord as easily as they could be with

Francis and the brothers on Mount Subasio. They had only to turn to the kingdom within. Francis had taught them that.

Although initially Clare may have followed Francis because she was a young girl infatuated with his dreams and talks of glory, once she and her sisters were alone at San Damiano, Francis grew smaller, though never less cherished in her heart. When she was left alone with love, he who is love emerged. And Clare discovered a whole new world of love and presence in Jesus.

She could always turn to him, frolic with him in the poppies or sit quietly with him long into the night. She could talk and ask his opinion, pray for people, be assured of Francis' and the brothers' love and support. Her Lord was always with her; in him a lifetime's worth of travel and excitement was wrapped up in daily meetings of deep contemplative prayer.

The room within her heart grew till all the brothers and the Poor Ladies, Francis and all the townspeople could fit into her once tiny cell, bursting its grill open as a soul content with listening love poured out its life and hope to the world. And a courtyard content with geraniums and swallows thrived from an inexhaustible well.

You leave the courtyard and look up at the facade of the church. There is a wooden door to the left of a small rose window. There are no steps to the door, no access except from within. This is the door that shut upon Clare di Favarone, the door that opened again upon the mercenary soldiers of the Emperor Frederick II to reveal the ciborium, that further enclosure where Clare lived behind the door within the golden cup with her Lover and Bridegroom. The door. The cup. Inside both you will begin your pilgrimage.

Inside San Damiano it is Clare's dual charism of

contemplation and healing that seep into the pilgrim soul. You pass through the small sanctuary where a door on the right enters into Clare's choir where the Poor Ladies offered up the fragrant perfume of their communal prayer. From there you ascend a narrow stairway past an ancient door that opens onto a small enclosed outdoor space believed to be the site of Clare's garden where Saint Francis first sang the "Canticle of the Creatures." A short distance beyond this small door is a tiny chapel that opens onto the dormitory of Saint Clare where the Poor Ladies slept and where Clare spent many years bedridden. Here, too, despite her illness, Clare ministered to her sisters in good times and bad, in sickness and in health.

At the far end of the open floor of the dormitory is the door where Clare stood when the monastery was under siege by the mercenary soldiers of Frederick II. Fearing for the lives and virginity of her sisters, Clare had the Blessed Sacrament brought. Then with the ciborium aloft at the open door, she challenged the aggressive, violent body of men, not with spirit, but with the *Body* of Christ. This gesture is central to the spirituality of Clare and Francis of Assisi. In Clare and Francis you now confront your residual Puritan-Jansenistic-Albigensian-Manichaean attitudes that manifest themselves in fear, mistrust, denigration of the human body.

At the time of Clare and Francis, Assisi was an Albigensian town, one of five hundred or so Albigensian strongholds in medieval Italy, and both saints had to counteract the attitudes they must surely have been influenced by as they grew up in their walled, self-absorbed city. To put it boldly, and perhaps to over-simplify as well, Albigensianism is the belief that matter is evil and spirit is good, and therefore we carry our souls around in "dirty" bodies which only death can liberate us from. We wouldn't ascribe to so "medieval" a creed. And yet how subtly Albigensian attitudes still creep into our modern lives.

We mention Albigensianism and point out that Clare holds the Body of Christ before the violent body of mercenary soldiers, because it is precisely here that your pilgrimage may falter. Can you, like Francis and Clare, convert the subtle anti-body attitudes of your life into an incarnational spirituality? Can you learn to love yourself, soul and body, as one integrated good?

## For Reflection

- *As he spoke to Francis from the crucifix at San Damiano, so Jesus has spoken to me at particular times, in particular places and in ways that I will always remember. I reflect now on one of those times, places, ways. How has this Jesus encounter affected my journey into the soul? my journey out into the community?*

- *What would I most like to learn from Saint Clare about cultivating love in my inner room? In what ways have I responded to (or ignored or neglected) my own call to be a contemplative?*

- *How do I feel about my body? How do I express my prayer and spirituality through my body? How am I reverencing this body of Jesus that I am? How might the Church encourage or guide us in developing a more incarnational spirituality?*

- *What will I do this week to help others love themselves as unique and irreplaceable members of the body of Christ?*

## Closing Prayer

### The Rooms of Saint Clare

Hers is the mystery of rooms.
The room from whose window she watches
Francis walk across the Piazza San Rufino
and into whose tapestried forest
                    she withdraws

to seek the unicorn's white horn
that brings her to that other room
where Bishop Guido places
the palm into her open soul.

Rooms open on rooms.
St. Mary of the Angels, the room of vows
that opens onto the nuns of Bastia,
the monastery on Mount Subasio, and
San Damiano with its rooms God has prepared for
    her,
each room conforming to the contours of her soul
like a fitted wedding dress.

There at San Damiano
she crosses the threshold
                    into the Royal Chamber.
Above the marble altar-bed
she sees herself in the mirror that spoke to Francis.
She's radiant, calm, pure with desire.
She kneels and the room
opens upon mansions of possibility:
other brides cross the threshold with her,
fill the rooms of their own espousals.
Rooms spill out into streets of their village,
a courtyard around whose well they gather
to draw water, talk their own domesticity.

They gather for church
            like women inside Assisi's
walls. They sing psalms, share the Bread of Life,
after which they pass
                a further threshold
into Lady Poverty's dining room where Clare
blesses another bread
                crossed with want and penance.

But it is the steep ascent from choir
through the narrow passageway
                    opening
into their Bridal Chamber
that lifts Clare and the Poor Ladies above routine.
For there is the room of redemptive suffering where
Clare ministers to her sick sisters,
lies bedridden sewing albs and altar linens.
There she opens the door, kneels
before her Eucharistic Lord, and
prays away the threatening advances
of the Emperor's mercenary soldiers.

There in the room of consummations
she holds her Rule that holds
all the rooms of the Poor Ladies' lives.
She presses the Book of Rooms to her heart and
crosses the final threshold into all the rooms
of her life
                now graced with him
who is the mirror she enters without effort,
without shattering the glass that
holds her image inside his.

Lord, there are many rooms in our lives. We walk through them towards you, in you, building a mansion of faith. Grace us with your image, let us see your face in the tasks of our everyday lives as you did for the Poor Ladies, be they tasks of sorrow or tasks of joy.

# DAY FOUR
## Saint Clare's Basilica

### Coming Together in the Spirit

*Clare died at San Damiano in 1253 with her sisters and Brothers Juniper and Leo at her side. Her body was brought from San Damiano to the church of San Giorgio, where Francis' body was also kept until the erection of his basilica. The Basilica of St. Clare was constructed on the exact site of the church of San Giorgio in 1257-60. The Romanesque-Gothic church was designed by Filippo di Campello. Like Francis', Clare's body rested in an unknown location beneath the church until the nineteenth century. Today it is preserved in a crystal casket in the crypt.*

The flame of Clare's spirit burned not only for her own warmth but for Francis and his dream. She was a living sacrifice, an offering given freely for anyone to come to and benefit from the heat and warmth of a heart aflame with love of God. Her name means "the bright and celebrated one," supposedly chosen by her mother, Ortolana, who received a message from God in prayer that the child would be a light to the whole world.

Clare's story is told very clearly in the lives of all who love. It is not people who are the mystery but love itself. And the living of that love is as varied as the starkness of San Damiano, the intimacy of the Portiuncula, the richness of the Basilica of St. Francis, the ethereal choir-song of the Basilica of St. Clare. The sweetness of that love is as tender as Mary Magdalene, as worried and anxious as Martha, and as patient and constant as the Lord's mother Mary. Clare outlived Francis by nearly thirty years. She remained faithful to the life of poverty— this Lady Poverty—until the end of her life.

## Defining Our Thematic Context

Saint Clare is a contemplative and a mystic. The way into her mystery is the way of mystical language, language like that of the Song of Songs. It is language that speaks of lover and beloved, bride and bridegroom. The way of the mystic is the way of poetry and metaphor and allegory which we embark upon on this fourth day of the retreat.

## Opening Prayer

And because the way and path is straight and the gate through which one passes and enters into life narrow (cf. Matthew 7:14), there are few who walk on it and enter through it. And if there are some who walk that way for a time, there are very few who persevere in it. How blessed are those to whom it it has been given to walk that way and persevere to the end!

Therefore, as we have set out on the path of the Lord, let us take care that we do not turn away from it by our own fault or negligence or ignorance nor that we offend so great a Lord and His Virgin Mother, and our father, the blessed Francis.... For this reason I bend my knees to the Father...that...the

Lord Himself Who has given a good beginning will
[also] give the increase and constant perseverance to
the end. Amen.—From the *Testament of St. Clare*[1]

# RETREAT SESSION FOUR

You leave San Damiano and ascend the hill to the
Porta Nuova, the new gate into the city of Assisi where
you arrive first at the Piazza of St. Clare. Across the town
and higher on the hill than the Piazza of St. Francis, the
Piazza of St. Clare and its basilica face the piazza and
basilica of Saint Francis in point, counterpoint fashion.

Two piazzas. Masculine and feminine.

Animus, anima. Two poles of the soul. This journey to
Assisi is to Francis and therefore to Clare, to Clare and
therefore to Francis, because, as Pope John Paul II said in
an improvised speech at the Proto-monastery of the Poor
Clares of Assisi on March 12, 1982:

> It is difficult to separate these two names, Francis
> and Clare. There is between them something very
> profound, which cannot be understood outside the
> criteria of Franciscan, Christian, Gospel
> spirituality....
>
> They were part of God's earthly creation. They
> were not something purely spiritual; they were not
> pure spirits. They had bodies; they were persons—
> and they were spirits. But in the living tradition of
> the Church, of all Christianity, of humanity, there
> remains not only the legend. There remains the way
> in which Francis saw his sister; the way in which he
> became united to Christ. He saw himself in her
> image, a bride of Christ, a mystical bride with whom

he shaped his holiness.[2]

The modern pilgrimage is toward reconciliation and integration of the male and female inside us all through the shared journey outside, which we make in a spirit of penance and anticipatory thanksgiving that we are women and men together on the way.

And so when you disembark at the upper piazza, that of Saint Clare, you plunge immediately into the mystical dimension of the heavenly Assisi where Clare is mother of all born or to be born of Lady Poverty, of whom Clare is the type and figure.

You enter the dark basilica of the Lady of Light, Clara, Chiara, Clare. She lies buried in the crypt, down the marble-walled passage to her bier. Her consuming, passionate love of God, a burning too hot for mortal flesh, has left her body charred and blackened beneath its waxed and cosmeticized shell.

The nun hides her own burning beneath a veil. She hands you a holy card and you kneel before the Lady Poverty's altar. What image stirs your pilgrim heart? There is an allegory about the Lady Poverty, entitled, *Sacrum Commercium*, the *Holy Exchange*, written circa 1227, that may be a catalyst for your understanding of how the early Franciscans spoke about Lady Poverty. In the allegory the antagonists are Lady Avarice and her handmaiden, Lady Sloth. Francis and the brothers go in search of the Lady Poverty, who dwells inside a high mountain, and they eventually bring her with them down from their caves at the Carceri further up Mount Subasio to where they dwell on the plain. The movement down in order to ascend, and the attendant anti-movements, like disarming in order to arm, stripping in order to clothe, renouncing in order to possess are the paradoxical juxtapositions that form the structure and meaning of what constitutes "perfect joy" in the Franciscan tradition:

The joy of poverty
is not to have nothing
in this world;
    the joy of poverty
is to have nothing
but God.

The allegory of the *Sacrum Commercium* takes these paradoxes and focuses them on the friars' relationship with the Lady Poverty. It begins with Francis pining for his lady like a love-struck troubadour, like the lover in the Song of Songs. "Francis [begins] to go about in the streets and crossings of the city, relentlessly, like a persistent hunter, diligently seeking whom his heart · [loves]."[3] But the people of the *city* don't understand him. "Sir, we do not know what you are saying. Speak to us in our own language and we will give you an answer."[4] Francis, therefore, leaves the city and goes to "a certain field, where he [sees] afar off two elderly men.... When blessed Francis approache[s] these men, he [says] to them, 'Tell me, I beg of you, where does Lady Poverty dwell, where does she feed, where does she lie at midday, for I am faint with love for her?' " The two men answer that "she has gone up into the mountain where God has directed her to go...."[5]

It is significant that Lady Poverty has not gone up onto the mountain, but into the mountain, a going into as into the womb, into the cave of Mount Subasio, from which Francis at the beginning of his conversion, had been re-born into a new relationship with God and creation.

The way to this Lady, who dwells in the mountain, the two men tell Francis, is to "remove the garments of your rejoicing...[and] take with you some faithful companions that you may listen to their advice as you go up the mountain and be strengthened by their help, for woe to the solitary man!" In the passage are foreshadowed two of the essentials elements of Franciscan spirituality: (1) removing the garments of your previous rejoicing, and (2) renouncing the solitary quest. The origins of these essential Franciscan gestures is, first of all, the passage in Saint Paul's Letter to the Phillipians, wherein he writes of Jesus Christ:

> Who, being in the form of God,
> did not count equality with God
> something to be grasped.
> But he emptied himself,
> taking the form of a slave,
> becoming as human beings are;
> and being in every way like a human being,
> he was humbler yet,
> even to accepting death, death on a cross.
> (Philippians 2:6-8, *The New Jerusalem Bible*)

Secondly, Christ's emptying himself of his divine attributes by dying on a cross like a human being makes community possible, for from the side of the crucified Christ is born the Church, the communion of the faithful. Francis and Clare and their companions embrace Lady Poverty as the Crucified Christ's spouse and widow and then go on the quest, not as solitary knights, but two-by-two on the road, as Jesus sent out his disciples two-by-two.

Two-by-two. You, pilgrim, can find these symbols and reflections in your world, your street, your longings. You can hear the music of the lovestruck troubadour, even if it is from the am/fm of the car next to you waiting anxiously at a stoplight while you are on your way to the grocery. You can find it most anywhere and usually by surprise. Once, in Assisi, there was an old *schwester*, or German nun, playing her handmade guitar. An old man with drab, baggy pants and an old cap shuffled on the sidewalk next to her. Each enjoyed and appreciated the other. Perhaps they remembered the old country. They were in no way embarrassed, though neither the dancing nor the playing was that good.

The songs Francis heard are still in Assisi, in the side streets and in the churches; but like every good piece of music, they must be listened to and appreciated for what they are, not for what they are not. Each person's interpretation will be unique, but every performance of the piece, expertly done or not, will bring great joy to the composer and the Creator. That is why Francis the troubadour was known to have fiddled an imaginary violin and heard beautiful masterpieces, pursuing Lady Poverty—and why the *schwester* saw a perfect polka and the shuffling old man heard a perfect tune.

## For Reflection

- *Who is Lady Poverty to me? What feelings does the devotion of Francis and Clare to Lady Poverty arouse in me? How does my own practice (to whatever degree) of voluntary poverty affect the world around me?*

- *How have I embraced both the male and female dimensions of my identity? How do I express the "two poles of my soul" in my prayer? ministry? relationships?*

- *Who are the faithful companions who have helped me to avoid the "solitary quest"? How have we guided, corrected, affirmed and supported one another in doing God's will?*

- *What will I do to experience more Franciscan joy in my everyday life? What music will I make for my sister and brother pilgrims—especially for those whose hearts need cheering?*

## Closing Prayer

Lord, help me find something noble and good to live for, some dream, some ideal. And let your will be made known to me through those I live with. May those I love inspire me to acts of charity and courage beyond my daily, sometimes boring, routine. And may the routine of my life itself be more than mechanical routine because I see your will in even the most humdrum actions of my life. Let everything ordinary in my life become extraordinary because it is done for you, Lord.

## Notes

[1] Clare of Assisi, *The Testament of St. Clare*, in *Francis and Clare: The Complete Works*, trans. and introduction by Regis Armstrong, O.F.M. Cap., and Ignatius Brady, O.F.M. (Mahwah, N.J.: Paulist Press, 1982), p. 232.

[2] *With Francis in the Church*, 116-118.

[3] *Sacrum Commercium*, in *Francis of Assisi: Omnibus of Sources*, ed. Marion Habig (Chicago: Franciscan Herald Press, 1972), p. 1553.

[4] Ibid.

[5] Ibid.

# DAY FIVE
## The Crucifix of San Damiano

### Coming Together in the Spirit

*The large crucifix of San Damiano is one of the most reproduced crucifixes in the world. It portrays a living Christ triumphant over death. It is painted in Byzantine style, probably from the late twelfth century, with figures surrounding Christ representing Calvary to heaven on the vertical axis and witnesses of the Passion to the whole of humanity on the horizontal axis, with Christ as the center. The strong iconesque colors are of red, black, and gold. Today the crucifix hangs in a side chapel of the Basilica of St. Clare.*

No one knows how the crucifix spoke to Francis. But it does not really matter; what matters is that it moved him to go and repair God's house which was falling into ruin. It is a strange crucifix. It has such life, as if it truly could speak. From the moment you step inside the chapel, its eyes are upon you; you can feel them everywhere in the room.

The crucifix hangs in a glass-covered case now, on a lime green velvet background. A light perpetually shines upon it. It leaves you wordless. Mere words could never capture what it communicates so loudly through the stillness. The corpus is frail. Hand-painted figures extend open palms to catch the flowing blood from Christ's hands and side and feet. But his face is serene. Almost totally indifferent to his state, he seems oblivious to all things except the person who is standing before him. His eyes do not look down in defeat nor pleadingly upward to God, but straight ahead, penetrating every other eye that meets his. He looks as if he is just ready to speak some profound secret, but he waits for you to speak first.

The artist, like Da Vinci, has captured the quizzical moment. To Francis, the lips parted and the moment spoke. And to all others who come here and sit in its presence another moment speaks, for someday all people must answer the question revealed—if only in speechless wonder and long searching glances held in the filtering of the light's burning rays.


## Defining Our Thematic Context

Like the ladies of a medieval castle Clare and the Poor Ladies of San Damiano were the brothers' inspiration as they preached and begged along the roads, knight-errants of the Great King. The tales of Arthur and his knights and Charlemagne and his paladins Clare heard in her father's palazzo next to the church of San Rufino. And when she entered the monastery of San Damiano she became the Poor Lady of the Castle, the Bride of the Poor, Crucified Savior.

This chivalric dimension makes of the Franciscan living-out of the gospel a tale full of heroism and courtesy and joy, virtues of the knights and ladies of chivalric lore. What today may seem extremes of poverty and deprivation were for Francis and Clare the stuff of heroic living-out of the gospel that paralleled the heroic exploits of knights and ladies of the secular court.

Clare's serving of her sisters, reversing the lady of the court's role of being served, democratized her Order of Poor Ladies; but at the same time the way Clare served was that of a true lady: with dignity and joy and a heroism that equaled that of Francis, the Knight of Christ.

The rituals of Clare's court were prayer and silence and contemplation. And when her lips' prayer ceased, her hands began their prayer, serving and working in the garden, and washing the feet of her sisters, ministering to the sick among them.

Hers also was the ministry of healing. Clare prayed over those whom Francis and the brothers sent her for healing prayer. Even today, eight centuries later, there continue to be healings in the dormitory of Saint Clare at San Damiano and at her tomb in the Basilica of St. Clare. In the early 1980's the taxi cab drivers of Assisi related how one of them drove a crippled man from the train station to Saint Clare's basilica and helped him down the steps to Saint Clare's tomb where the man asked to be left alone to pray. The cab driver joined his fellow drivers for a cappuccino at the bar overlooking the fountain in the Piazza of St. Clare. Some time later the man emerged from the Basilica and danced around the piazza healed of his lameness. The drivers made the Sign of the Cross and asked forgiveness for their jaded hearts that had forgotten what manner of city Assisi really is.

## Opening Prayer

The affection of Jesus holds one fast;
his contemplation is like a breath of new life.
His kindness fills one to the brim;
his sweetness is in overflowing measure.

The recollection of him shines with a soft light.
His fragrance revives the dead.
The glorious vision of him is beatific happiness
to all the citizens of heavenly Jerusalem.

Now, since he is the splendor of eternal glory
and brightness of everlasting light
and the mirror without spot (Wisdom 7:26),
look steadfastly into his mirror every day.

See in it every time you look—and look into it
always—your own face.
This will urge you to vest yourself totally,
within and without,
with adornments of all the virtues (Psalm 44:10).[1]

Lord, Jesus, may my contemplation of you have no other
goal than conversion, interior transformation, so that I
may become a mirror, reflecting something of your face
for all my brothers and sisters.

# RETREAT SESSION FIVE

The most significant ritual of Clare's court was the
Poor Ladies at their mirror. Theirs was not the mirror of
the ladies of the court, looking to see themselves as they
were seen by men, posing to be attractive for lords and
knights.

The Poor Ladies' mirror was the crucifix in which they
saw him into whose image they were merging. They
looked not to see how they were seen; they looked to see
how he is seen, the Bridegroom made perfect and
beautiful in love poured out for love of their love. "See
what I have done to make myself perfect for you; it is

what you will do to make yourself my perfect bride; it is what you are already becoming."

Clare described for her sisters what they would see in the Mirror who is the Poor Christ if they looked there daily:

In this mirror you will find poverty in bright reflection. You will see humility and love beyond words. You will be able to see this clearly with the grace of God and to contemplate it in its fullness.

Fix your attention first to what has prime place in the mirror, and this is the poverty of the babe who is placed in the manger and wrapped in swaddling clothes. What tremendous humility we find here and what astounding poverty! The king of angels and the lord of heaven and earth is resting in a manger. In the center of the mirror consider long and carefully the humility which walks side by side, with blessed poverty, and the countless labors and hardships which he bore for the redemption of the human race. And, finally, in studying the last features of the mirror, open your mind and your soul to the unspeakable love which prompted him to want to suffer on the gibbet of the cross and there to die the shameful kind of death. Let us give our full attention to what the same mirror, placed on the wood of the cross, sets before the eyes of all who pass by: 'Oh all you pass by the way, attend and see if there be any sorrow like my sorrow.' Let me answer with one voice and one spirit him who calls out and laments: 'I recall in my soul and my heart grows faint within me' (Lamentations 1:12 and 3:20). When you respond in this way, each time you will be caught up more mightily in the circle of love, O queen of the heavenly king.[2]

It is hard for us today to look at such a Christ and not

suspect that we are somehow masochistic to do so, that we are making of the contemplation of Christ an exercise in self-hatred and self-punishment for secret sin. But such is not the case. The Mirror of Christ is the mirror of what we continue to witness daily in the horrors of the eve of the twenty-first century. In Christ's face, that face is redeemed which otherwise would remain so horrible it would have to be denied in favor of some sweet-looking, cosmeticized Christ. The face which Christ Crucified mirrors and redeems is translated by Nicholas Carpenter in his poem, "Terminus."

> Here is a piece of required reading
> at the end of our century
> the end of a millennium that began with the
>     Crusades
>
> The transcript of an interview
> between a Red Cross doctor
> and a Muslim girl in Bosnia
> twelve years old
> who described her rape by men
> calling themselves soldiers
> different men every night one after the other
> six seven eight of them
> for a week
> while she was chained by the neck
> to a bed in her former schoolhouse....[3]

That is what men continue to do; that is what men did to Christ, and in his enduring it, he redeemed and bequeathed the face of God to those like the Bosnian girl, like the numberless women and men of all wars, of all victims of hatred and revenge. In voluntary solidarity with those women, with the Christ whose mirror they are, Clare and the Poor Ladies offered their pure and chaste lives in expiation with Christ; they embraced with their own poverty the Poor Christ.

Given the horrors of history, the horrors of our own time, only a tough-minded and tough-willed love like that of Francis and Clare is credible. Life that is sweetness and light without any reaching out to the continuing crucified face of Christ is a Pollyana religion without depth and without compassion. And it is compassion that is the hallmark of the spirituality of both Clare and Francis. Compassion, in its root meaning of "suffering with." They suffer with their crucified Lord who in turn is the suffering of all humankind stamped upon the face of God. God's face is human, Jewish, falsely accused, mocked, spit upon, tortured and left to die a slow suffocating death. Such is the mark of the "beast" of evil that Carpenter names in a further stanza:

> 1993 may as well be 1943
> and it should be clear now
> that the beast in his many guises
> the flags and vestments
> in which he wraps himself
> and the elaborate titles he assumes
> can never be outrun[4]

It *seems* he cannot, anyway. And his guises are all human. Human beings crucified Christ, human beings continue to crucify him; and human beings are the face of the crucified Christ. But if this same Christ be not risen, as Saint Paul writes, then Francis and Clare and all of us are fools to care; best to close our eyes and refuse to see what does not touch us directly. But if Christ is indeed risen from the dead and we do follow him, then everything done here fashions the face we will wear there: not the face of the beast raging eternally in hatred and self-absorbed guilt, but the face of the crucified Christ transformed now into the radiant, joyful face of the person each one of us becomes in fixing our eyes on the face of God.

On retreat we learn to look at the crucified face of Christ and see our own and the faces of all who suffer with him. That suffering-with is the pledge of our transformation into the resurrected Christ become the new mirror of those who love to the end.

The reason Christ crucified moves to the foreground of Francis' and Clare's life is not a maudlin love of death, of the macabre. It is that the face of Christ they see around them is for the most part poor, rejected, emaciated. Both Francis and Clare live from childhood on in wealth and comparative luxury. They do not have to see beyond that world, but their seeing is long. They both have vision, that grace of seeing that draws them out of their own narrow world to the larger reality that borders the safety of their own comfort and security. Because they see what others don't see or refuse to see, they recognize the mirror of their vision in Christ crucified. All these poor, rejected human beings, the lepers and outcasts of society are somehow Christ. And only in reaching out to the poor and embracing their poverty can they find Christ and can the poor begin to be transformed into the image of another Christ, the resurrected Christ whose face shines in those who have been embraced and loved by saints.

The world wears a crucified face before love turns its eyes on it. The look of love is the beginning of transformation. In the words of Saint Clare in the same letter to Agnes of Prague: "Take a long, loving look also at the delights which cannot be described in words and which he brings to you, and the riches, and the honors that have no dateline to end them. Responding to the greatness of all this, with all the fullness of desire of which your heart is capable and the love that it can summon, shout out in joy: 'Draw me! After you we shall run in the odor of your ointments, heavenly bridegroom! I shall run, lest I faint, until you lead me in to the storeroom, until your left hand is under my head and until your right arm will happily embrace me, and you will kiss me with the most joyful kiss of your mouth.'"[5]

## For Reflection

- *What am I doing to repair God's house today? How do I (or will I) share this work with other pilgrims?*

- *When do I experience solidarity with the suffering body of Christ in our world today? In what ways am I (or will I be) a healing presence to them?*

- *When I focus on a crucifix in prayerful attention, what do I see in the mirror? How does what I see call me to self-examination? reconciliation? conversion? compassion?*

- *How might Francis and Clare help me to see more clearly and often the face of Christ in those I live with and in those I find it most difficult to love?*

## Closing Prayer

### Saint Clare Dies at Her Mirror, August 11, 1253

I've lived in the labyrinth, love its scrubbed walls, doors whose thresholds lead to the brass basin, worn where a sister's foot soaks warm in my loving hand. Portals here billow into linen albs, their shadows arching into gates through which Saracen horses pound toward their own retreat; the blinding ciborium whirls

warriors, spins our lacing bobbins. Winter roofbeams
groan their vows beneath God's weight, His rough beard
scratches the eaves like a storm of olive branches.

I've embraced the labyrinth, the basin's womb become
a mirror for seeing around corners; looked into, it's
the crucifix that spoke to Francis, Christ's wounded,
bent face now a lucid window into my own riddle
recumbent on the stone pillow. On the roof God hops,
sparks in a gossip of sparrows. Small, brown, winged,
my soul flits through death's dark mirror, into light.

## Notes

[1] Fourth Letter of Clare to Agnes of Prague.

[2] Fourth Letter of Clare to Agnes of Prague, trans. David Temple, O.F.M., in *Clare, A Light in the Garden* (Cincinnati: St. Anthony Messenger Press, 1992), pp. 95-96.

[3] Nicholas Carpenter, "Terminus," *The Best Poetry of 1995*, ed. Richard Howard and David Lehman (New York: Touchstone, 1995), pp. 37-38.

[4] Ibid., pp. 38-39.

[5] Letter to Agnes, in *Clare, A Light in the Garden*, p. 96.

# DAY SIX
## Saint Francis' Basilica

### Coming Together in the Spirit

*Francis died on the evening of October 3, 1226, at the Portiuncula. The building of his basilica was initiated by Brother Elias, Francis' successor as minister general, under the direct order of Pope Gregory IX to raise a triumphant structure to glorify the gospel poverty of Saint Francis. On May 25, 1230, Brother Elias placed Francis' body in a secret crypt to ensure that no one would steal the saint's remains. The basilica is a treasure of paintings, frescoes and mosaics, the most famous artists being Giotto, Lorenzetti and Cimabue. The plan of the church is a double T (the tau symbol), forming an upper and lower church; underneath is the crypt where Saint Francis is buried.*

Francis' basilica is truly an architectural fortress built of pink and white stone: two superimposed churches above the crypt where Francis is buried.

In Francis' day the site of the basilica was a potters' field where dead criminals and the bodies of the poor whose families could not afford burial were thrown over the city wall to waste away in the sun. Some wish that Francis, too, could have been buried like them, the poor and marginal people he loved, a small wooden cross marking his grave. Then in death as in life he would have been little and poor.

But we do not blame Brother Elias for agreeing to build this basilica. He was trying to do what he thought was best to protect the body of Saint Francis and to be obedient to the Holy See, as Francis himself directed his brothers to be.

Brother Elias hid Francis' body, burying it deep in the bowels of the basilica, so the rival towns of Perugia and Rome would not try to steal it away or other towns come and strew the relics all over Italy.

Instead, the Basilica of St. Francis becomes *the* reliquary, one of the great reliquaries of Christendom, filled with stunning art that heralds the beginning of the Renaissance.

## Defining Our Thematic Context

Pilgrimage is quest is retreat. Retreat is pilgrimage is quest. And this dynamic both affects and is enacted on the dual geography of nature and soul, an interior and exterior landscape. Nature, the exterior landscape, embraces not only the world "out there," removed from me, but the body, as well. We use the word "embrace" to imply the reverence with which the pilgrim, the questor, the retreatant is to approach body, soul, nature. All are good, all partake of the geography of the other. The journey into one's soul is also a bodily journey. The journey into nature is a journey into the geography of one's own body and soul. Unity. Not division. Oneness. Not dichotomy.

## Opening Meditation

Today there is nothing, can be nothing, in Assisi but the memory of him who took Lady Poverty to wife. Yet the city we see but little resembles what it was in Francis' day. What we see is not what he saw, but is, in fact, his creation. The city S. Francis knew had no San Francesco, no Sacro Convento, no Santa Chiara and no Rocca towering over all....

And yet one finds oneself on his account wandering up and down the steep and climbing ways, through street and piazza where he played as a child, where he went gaily as a young man, which presently saw him begging his bread, and echoed alike with the scorn of his fellows and the irresistible words of his preaching. Here is the house, here is the stable, in which he was born; here the font in which he was baptised. Just beyond the walls is San Damiano where the Crucifix spoke to him. Here before Santa Maria Maggiore he stripped himself and repudiated his earthly father, Pietro Bernardone. There is the house of his first companion, Bernard of Quintavalle. And there in the Vescovado he lay till they bore him out of Porta Moiano on his last journey when he turned and blessed the city he loved, but could no longer see, on the way to S. Mary of the Angels, where he was to die. And finally, here in the great triple church dedicated in his honor, on the Collis Inferni, now the Collis Paradisi, we may venerate his dust....

San Francesco is the grandiose tomb of the little poor man, who should have been buried in the lee of some wood where birds sing and the earth is carpeted with primroses.[1]

Saint Francis, I know that your real monument was your life and example, the brothers and sisters you left behind, the Rule of Life you gave those who would follow you. Help me to follow in your footsteps by striving to live the gospel instead of building monuments to myself. And may my living of the gospel make a difference among those I live with and bring goodness and peace to the town I live in.

# RETREAT SESSION SIX

As Henry James keenly observed, the Basilica of St. Francis is "intended perhaps [as] an image between heart and head.... For by way of doing something supremely handsome and impressive the sturdy architects of the thirteenth century piled temple upon temple and bequeathed a double version of their idea. The luminescence of Giotto's frescoes in the upper church's 'well-ordered head' are made more brilliant by way of passage into and through the lower church."[2]

The Basilica of St. Francis which, as James indicates, is really two churches, one built upon another (three churches if you include the crypt chapel where Francis is buried), a medieval analogue of the journey of the soul from darkness to light, the dynamic of the inner depths of a spiritual retreat. There are doubtless such archetypal analogues in all religions, but your journey to Assisi effects in the end a familiarity with this twofold church of Saint Francis as an apt image of the inner, subterranean workings of the soul on spiritual retreat. We sprinkle this chapter with the words of Henry James whose aspergil like a verbal wand is most apt to hit the mark, and anoint what is seen with the life-giving grace of his precise seeing. Writing of the lower church, James observes:

For the first minutes after leaving the clearer gloom you catch nothing but a vista of low black columns closed by the great fantastic cage surrounding the altar, which is thus placed, by your impression, in a sort of gorgeous cavern. Gradually you distinguish details, become accustomed to the penetrating chill, and even manage to make out a few frescoes; but the general effect remains splendidly sombre and subterranean. The vaulted roof is very low and the pillars dwarfish, though immense in girth, as befits pillars supporting substantially a cathedral. The tone of the place is a triumph of mystery, the richest harmony of lurking shadows and dusky corners, all relieved by scattered images and scintillations.

The darkness of vaults and side-chapels is overwrought with vague frescoes, most of them by Giotto and his school, out of which confused richness the terribly distinct little faces characteristic of these artists stare at you with a solemn formalism. Some are faded and injured, and many so ill-lighted and ill-placed that you can only glance at them with decent conjecture; the great group, however—four paintings by Giotto on the ceiling above the altar—may be examined with some success. Like everything of that grim and beautiful master they deserve examination; but with the effect ever of carrying one's appreciation in and in, as it were, rather than of carrying it out and out, off and off, as happens for us with those artists who have been helped by the process of 'evolution' to grow wings. This one, 'going in' for emphasis at any price, stamps hard, as who should say, on the very spot of his idea—thanks to which fact he has a concentration that has never been surpassed....[3]

What "stamps hard," in Henry James' words, are four frescoes called the Vaults of Paradise, above the high altar in the lower church of the basilica. They are hard to see in the semi-darkness of the lower church, so unlike the lightsome Giotto frescoes of the upper church. Generally believed to be painted by Giotto, this group of frescoes decorates the ceiling of the room directly above Francis' tomb and was intended to be the most splendid work in the basilica. Three of the rectangular frescoes show the vows of poverty, chastity and obedience. The fourth portrays Francis in glory, surrounded by angels and dressed in a rich deacon's dalmatic.

In this allegory of Holy Poverty, Lady Poverty is the bride and Francis the groom. She has thorn bushes at her feet; their straggly stems wind up and around her body and blossom into delicate roses at her head. Jesus stands between them giving Francis her hand like a proud father giving his most cherished daughter away.

Woman and symbol, bride and dream—as you have seen on your pilgrimage/retreat, for Francis poverty was the most beautiful, worthy lady any knight ever fought for. Her battlegrounds, the leper colony and the muddied streets, were more noble to him than the field of battle. The mud of Rivotorto and the cold, penetrating dampness of mountain caves became the silken tents of the most extravagant tournament. Francis sang her love songs in the night and searched for joy and comfort in her bosom. She was his lady.

All of which sounds glorious and romantic. But, is such a love affair possible for you, pilgrim? How can you experience in your life, on the eve of the twenty-first century, something of the joy and peace and enthusiasm for God that Francis and Clare experienced? The present successor of Saint Francis as minister general of the Franciscans, Fr. Hermann Schaluck, gives us a way we can experience the perfect joy of Saint Francis. Fr. Hermann offers us a modern reading of the gospel story of the Good Samaritan:

> A certain man went down from Jerusalem to Jericho,
> and fell among thieves, which stripped him of his
> raiment, and wounded him, and departed, leaving
> him half dead:
>    And by chance there came down a certain priest
> that way; and when he saw him, he passed by on the
> other side.
>    And likewise a Levite, when he was at the place,
> came and looked on him, and passed by on the other
> side.
>    But a certain Samaritan, as he journeyed, came
> where he was; and when he saw him, he had
> compassion on him.
>    And went to him, and bound up his wounds,
> pouring in oil and wine, and set him on his own
> beast, and brought him to an inn, and took care of
> him.
>    And on the morrow when he departed, he took
> out two pence, and gave them to the host, and said
> unto him, Take care of him; and whatsoever thou
> spendest more, when I come again, I will repay thee.
> (Luke 10:30-36)[4]

Brother Hermann points out that in the fourfold ministry
of the Samaritan there is (1) contemplative seeing,
(2) affective response, (3) practical caring and
(4) sustained assistance, all of which Saint Francis taught
and lived out in his ministry to the lepers, the poor and
marginated, the outcasts of thirteenth-century Umbria.

But this contemplative seeing does not just happen. It
is born out of the kind of prayerful retreat/pilgrimage
you have made in these pages and in the silence and
solitude of your own imagination by meditating on the
meaning of the story of Francis and Clare. You have

entered these words and placed yourself in the world of Francis and Clare of Assisi. There you have prayed and asked yourself how you could go and do as they did: love God in the poor, in nature, in your own life. Meditating in this way, with an eye and ear toward doing something in your own life to follow in their footsteps, differentiates this kind of meditation from simple imaginative identification with or re-creation of an historical event. Contemplative *seeing* leads to *affective response*. You are moved somehow; you are touched with remorse, or compassion, or love. And this movement of the heart leads you to *practical caring* that is merely faddish or transitory self-indulgence if there is not *sustained assistance*—that following-through in charity that is the test of true love, of the Divine dimension of your good works. It is the following-through on your good intentions, your charitable impulses, that transforms both yourself and those you try to love. And it is that following-through that leads you back into the silence and solitude of retreat where you can listen to the inner meaning of things again. There you enter a sacred space where you are moved again to contemplative seeing that elicits a response of charity and compassion.

So, in a sense, you go on retreat to learn again how to live, to be inspired and moved to live for something more than your own selfish impulses. To be a part of something bigger than yourself and to live a more interior life.

The interior life. The words are dangerous for a retreatant when they are not balanced by pilgrimage, by taking to the road again like Francis. And this does not mean that you have to be a do-gooder, a religious bore who intrudes on others' solitude to get them to do what you know is best for them.

What then does this taking to the road with Francis mean? Again, Fr. Hermann Schaluck instructs us: It means, "a contemplative encounter with reality, with the men and women of our time. It is allowing one's heart, mind and emotions to be touched by what one sees. Prayer is doing the good one can do with his/her own talents, time, and opportunities. It learns how to create a community which will sustain the good which we have begun." It involves, "through God's grace, the respectful and compassionate look at our world, our reality, our neighbors, the poor, creation."[5]

Respectful, compassionate. How often we pass one another with vinegar on our lips, with dismissal, indifference or contempt in our eyes. We are not seeing with contemplative eyes. We need to retreat to a space, a quiet, where we can find our own eyes again, where we can learn to see ourselves and others and our world as they really are.

And this seeing, no matter how innocent or endearing it may be, is not contemplative seeing unless the affective response it elicits leads to practical caring, which may be caring for yourself, learning again to see like a child or perhaps just learning to see a child again.

Sometimes the most practical caring is of the child in you, of the interior person who has not been tended to for a long time. And this child, this "other" self is very likely not some innocent, some precious little thing, but some undeveloped part of the psyche that is a child only in that it has never been allowed to have its say.

Speaking to or out of a part of yourself illustrates graphically that your silent pilgrimage is not a silence that is an absence of all sound, and your solitude is not loneliness. The silence you have experienced on this pilgrimage/retreat has involved the diminution of outer noise, it is true; but the inner speaking of the heart has still been there, the voices that rise to consciousness from within you.

Granted, many traditions endeavor to still inner voices, to become completely quiet, all-listening to something other than the chatter of your own *mind*. But this is not the kind of inner voices we are talking about here. What is meant is the murmurings of the *heart*, the images that rise from the deepest center of the self, the voice of the soul from which and to which the divine speaks.

And you know this inner voice, the voice of the soul, by no other test than the test of compassion and true charity: affective response that leads to practical caring for both yourself and others, a caring that is not just a passing fancy, a feel-good, one-shot doing, but a sustained following-through.

The voice that leads only to further introspection, to self-improvement at the expense of others, especially the poor and marginated, the outcast and lonely, is full of delusion and does not ring true. To love what is difficult to love and to persevere therein, leads to God. That is the lesson of Francis and Clare. That is where this short but long journey from the Assisi train station to the basilicas of Francis and Clare has brought you. The horizontal journey to a place of prayer and solitude is simultaneously a vertical journey into your heart of hearts, the dwelling place of the *Altissimu omnipotente, bon Signore*, the Most High, Good God.

## For Reflection

- *As I contemplate my own death, what "monument" do I hope to be remembered by? How might following in the footsteps of Francis and Clare lead me to that goal?*

- *What images—in nature, art or architecture, literature or*

*everyday life—might I contemplate in order to come to a*
*deeper appreciation of Lady Poverty?*

- *How will I join with other pilgrims and disciples in*
  *practicing the fourfold ministry of the Good Samaritan (as*
  *outlined by Fr. Hermann Schaluck)? How do I hope to be*
  *transformed by faithfulness to this process?*

- *What has the voice of my soul been saying to me during this*
  *pilgrimage-retreat? How will I attend to that voice?*

## Closing Prayer

Though Saint Francis had to moderate his early
rigor because of his illness, he continued to say: "My
brothers and sisters, let us begin to serve the Lord
God, for up to now we have done little, or
nothing."—Celano, *First Life*, 103

Lord, let us never become stagnant in our desire to serve
you. Let us not be complacent or rest on our past services
or successes. But let us strive to radiate outward,
beginning with our own souls, our child within, our
neighbors and those along the road, until we lie face up
staring at the vaults of paradise you prepare for us at the
hour of our death.

### Notes

[1] Edward Hutton, *Assisi and Umbria Revisited* (New York: David
McKay Company, Inc., 1953), pp. 1-3.

[2] "Italian Hours" in *Henry James: Collected Travel Writings, The
Continent* (New York: Library of America, 1993), pp. 498-499.

[3] Ibid., pp. 499-500.

[4] A talk by Fr. Hermann Schaluck, quoted in *Francisco*, Newsletter of the Province of Our Lady of Guadalupe, August, 1992.

[5] Ibid.

# DAY SEVEN
# Saint Clare's Garden

### Coming Together in the Spirit

*On the second story of San Damiano there is a small opening leading from the inside stairway through the wall out onto a small, secluded balcony called the Garden of St. Clare. During his illness in the spring of 1225, Francis came to San Damiano to rest and be cared for by Clare and the Poor Ladies. In his suffering he composed the "Canticle of Brother Sun," a song of praise to all God's creation. Francis may have been carried on a litter to be warmed by the sun on this balcony, or he may have composed the "Canticle" in a makeshift hut beside San Damiano's walls. A bronze plaque on the balcony wall commemorates the traditional site of the "Canticle's" composition.*

The space where Francis wrote the "Canticle of Brother Sun" is so small. You have to duck through a little opening in the wall to get to it; once inside you find it only measures about five by eight feet. Red geraniums decorate it and Brother Sun bathes them with his love; they seem to grow very well. It is bright and sunny in this niche. Other legends say Francis wrote the "Canticle" in the darkness of a little twig hut that Clare had made for him outside her cloister walls.

The "Canticle" is a symbol of total integration

between creature and Creator, like a fish in the sea and the sea in the fish. Francis saw all things touched by the hand of God and addressed them as brothers and sisters.

All of creation was united through the presence of the Holy Trinity, which became to him the banner of his heavenly family's heritage and the noblest of all coats-of-arms. Francis knew the secret of such unity. To be united was to be constantly and consciously present to the other as Francis was to his Lord and the Lord is to all creation. Francis' love of the Trinity was always on his lips, in his heart and in his mind. He began all his prayers with its praise and sought its unity and perfection in all that he did. That meant to be as uncomplicated as a circle but as integrated as a spiral.

To Francis creation was the outreach of the spiral from and through his Lord. Every creature became sacred because it flowed from God. God gave Francis the sensitivity to realize this fact to the point of feeling total oneness with something as tenuous as the wind. Water and fire, wind and earth became his home and family. And all living creatures became his brothers and sisters.

In this knowledge he became totally free to live as a beggar or talk to a wolf or a bird, to sing to a poppy or embrace a leper, to call God his own father and to stand naked in the streets. For Francis knew he was at home with all creation and all creation knew it was at home with Saint Francis.

## Defining Our Thematic Context

Though you, pilgrim, have toured the piazzas and basilicas of Francis and Clare, you long, like so many pilgrims before you, to return now to San Damiano outside the walls of Assisi. Why? Perhaps because these other places are big and formidable, crowded, touristy, and you long for simplicity, some unity to all the dichotomies unfolding and dancing in your head. You begin to understand that at San Damiano Clare and Francis are one, in a way they are not one inside the walls, where each has her or his own basilica. At San Damiano the spirits of Francis and Clare dwell together, just as they both once lived there bodily. Francis himself was drawn to San Damiano after he received the stigmata on Mount La Verna. It was like coming home to sing his final song with a grateful heart.

### Opening Prayer

Lord, we enter into the mystery of your Incarnation. Because you took on humanity, everything about us is redeemed. All of nature bears the mark of your footprint, as Saint Francis made us aware. He praised you, Lord, through and for all that you have made. We pray that your Incarnation will so fill our hearts and minds that we will embrace all things as good and redeemed by your life among us, your Resurrection from the dead.

# RETREAT SESSION SEVEN

Detachment. One of those misleading words. You read the saints' lives, their words. Detachment is central, prior to experiencing union with God. If God is to find you, you must be without attachment to things, people, ideas, other than God. And so, wrongly, you may begin to "detach" yourself by withdrawing, removing yourself, abdicating responsibility to and for the world around you. You may even enter upon a journey that is nothing more than the short distance between *yourself* attached and *yourself* detached—*you* still at the center.

You may even, through an extreme inversion of reality, begin to see things and people and, in short, anything material, as evil, as coming from an evil god, who is the source of matter, as the good God is deemed the source of spirit. Detachment, improperly understood, can lead to this kind of dualism, and has actually done so throughout the history of Western spirituality, from Manichaeism to Albigensianism to Jansenism. As you learned earlier in the retreat, it was, in fact, Albigensianism that permeated the Italian city-states at the time of Saint Francis. His own city of Assisi was an Albigensian stronghold. And how extraordinary, how full of genius was Saint Francis' response.

Instead of withdrawing from the material world, he entered into a whole new relationship with that world that resulted in a profound detachment in the truest theological sense of that word. He relinquished, not things, but control and power over them in favor of a fraternal relationship which enabled him to call all things "brother" and "sister." Instead of removing himself from material reality, he entered into all things, praising God for them, with them, in them, by means of them, and through them. He never spoke of "things," nor even of "possessions" as evil. Evil, as he put it, was *appropriatio*, appropriation of things material or spiritual, making of them objects of ownership and control and dominance. For everything is given us, lent by the Great Almsgiver, the Most High, All-Powerful Good Lord, who made all things, material and spiritual. In the twenty-third chapter of the *Rule of 1221*, a chapter that could be entitled, "A Franciscan Manifesto," Francis writes:

Almighty, most high and supreme God, Father, holy
and just, Lord, King of heaven *and* earth, we give
you thanks for yourself. Of your own holy will you
created all things spiritual *and* physical, made us in
your own image and likeness, and gave us a place in
paradise, through your only Son, in the Holy Spirit.[1]

That was in 1221, almost at the beginning of the
Franciscan movement. Later, in 1224, after receiving the
stigmata of the crucified Christ, after descending the holy
mountain of La Verna, after more than fifty days in the
darkness of his blindness, in extreme pain and
disillusionment over his brothers' abandonment of Lady
Poverty in the building of monasteries, after lying on the
ground of San Damiano those same fifty days with field
mice running over his broken, emaciated body, Francis
hears a voice:

"Tell me, Brother: if, in compensation for your
suffering and tribulations you were given an
immense and precious treasure: the whole mass of
the earth changed into pure gold, pebbles into
precious stones, and the waters of the rivers into
perfume, would you not regard the pebbles and the
waters as nothing compared to such a treasure?
Would you not rejoice?" Blessed Francis answered:
"Lord, it would be a very great, very precious and
inestimable treasure beyond all that one can love
and desire!" "Well, Brother," the voice said, "be
glad and joyful in the midst of your infirmities and
tribulations: as of now, live in peace as if you were
already sharing my kingdom."[2]

Which, of course, was what Francis had been doing all
along, "sharing" God's kingdom, which, because of
Francis' unique relationship to it, was indeed already

transformed into "pure gold, precious stones, perfume."

It is after hearing this voice, in his extreme illness and blinded of all light, except that which was within, that Francis sings the "Canticle of the Creatures" in Clare's garden, a poem which reveals the depths of his union with all of creation through which he attains his own final integration. But here you must stop and back up. This is the end of the story that needs to be told before the song can be sung.

The spontaneous singing of the "Canticle of the Creatures" is dreamlike and reveals the structure of Francis' unconscious mind, not the conscious, ordering mind.

The struggle, the making, for Francis of Assisi was of the life, not of the poem. The "Canticle" is a spontaneous singing (overflow, if you like) out of a life whose structure and order is revealed in the marvelous order of the poem, even though Francis did not sit down to deliberately order the words on paper. In other words, Francis' poem is the spontaneous singing of what was received in the struggle, the surrender, the waiting in darkness for images to flood the conscious mind, images welling up from the unconscious, revealing (as on a map) the order which the psyche has become through prayer and unselfish love.

Francis' transformation to singing bird, the lark he loved so well, is what sets him apart from the modern metamorphosis, that descent into creatures that is a denigration, a humiliation and defeat, rather than a descent that is an ascent, the way down becoming the way up, as in Christ's descent into the tomb, into hell to harrow it, rising through layers of oppression and murder and genocide into the light of Easter morning, trailing those who would rise with him.

Francis' poem takes the four elements of the universe,

earth, water, air and fire and puts them into the binary sexual combinations of Brother Sun and Sister Moon, Brother Fire and Sister Water, Brother Air and Sister Earth our mother. All the elements are enclosed between a male sun and a female earth reminiscent of the Chinese yin and yang. The male and female pairs seem to be concrete images of the integration of the Jungian animus and anima in the soul. In embracing all the combinations of male and female in the cosmos, Saint Francis is embracing the male and female dimensions of his soul.

For the Franciscan, Eloi Leclerc, the "Canticle of the Creatures" is not primarily a song of external nature, but of the soul expressed through dreamlike images of the natural world.[3] In embracing the four elements of the universe, pairing them sexually, and praising God through, with, and for them, Saint Francis is really embracing dreamed images of the four elements, images that rise as archetypes from the depths of his own soul. For to praise God through the cosmos is to praise God in the soul. As someone once said, every landscape we love is the landscape of our own soul.

When you close your eyes and pray, what images rise to your consciousness? Probably they are images of Jesus and Mary, the saints and angels, images, in other words that come from art, from the pictures you have seen. When Francis prayed, the mystery of the Incarnation was so deeply impressed on his soul that he praised God through images of nature made holy because of Jesus. Sister Earth was holy because Jesus walked upon the earth; Sister Water was holy because Jesus went down into the Jordan to be baptized by John; Brother Air was holy because Jesus breathed the air and breathed out his last breath on the cross; Brother Fire was holy because Jesus said that he came to cast fire on the earth.

We praise God through images derived from art;

Francis praised God through images derived from
nature. In that sense Saint Francis was a romantic: he let
nature sing through him. He was not a romantic in the
naive sense of a lover of nature who sees nature as good
and human beings as evil.

And this is what he sang, this Francis, this wholly
Incarnational poet:

Highest, all-powerful, good Lord,
Yours is the praise, the glory, and the honor,
And every blessing.
They belong to you alone, Most High,
And no one is worthy to speak your name.

So, praised be you, my Lord, with all your creatures,
Especially Sir Brother Sun,
Who makes the day and enlightens us through you.
He is lovely and radiant and grand;
And he heralds you, his Most High Lord.

Praised be you, my Lord, through Sister Moon
And the Stars.
You have hung them in heaven shining and precious
    and fair.

And praise to you, my Lord, through Brother Wind,
Through air and cloud, calm, and every weather
That sustains your creatures.

Praised be you, My Lord, through Sister Water,
So very useful and humble and precious and chaste.

Yes, and praise to you, my Lord, through Brother
    Fire.
Through him you illumine our night,

And he is handsome and jocund, robust and strong.

Praised be you, My Lord, through our Sister Mother
    Earth,
Who nourishes us and teaches us,
Producing all kinds of fruits and colored flowers and
    herbs.

O, and praise to you, my Lord,
Through those who forgive one another in your love
And who bear sickness and trials.
Blessed are they who live on in peace,
For they will be crowned by you, Most High!

Praise to you, my Lord, through our Sister Bodily
    Death,
From whom no one living can escape.
How dreadful for those who die in sin,
How lovely for those who are found in your Most
    Holy Will,
For the second death can do them no harm.

O praise and bless my Lord,
Thank him and serve him
Humbly but grandly!


## For Reflection

- *How does Saint Francis enable me to understand the
  meaning of authentic detachment? How do I most need to
  practice this virtue?*

- *In what ways have I, during times of illness, deprivation,
  grief or great pain, experienced enlightenment? What*

*difference did these experiences of enlightenment make in my relationship with God? with others?*

- *What images might I use if I were to compose my own canticle? How might I reflect the male and female dimensions of my soul? Where might my San Damiano be?*

- *How will I keep this retreat with Francis and Clare alive in my prayer life? family or community life? ministry?*

- *Where might my pilgrim heart lead me in the years ahead?*

## Closing Prayer

In the morning when the sun rises, everybody ought to praise God, who created the sun for our benefit; through it our eyes get the light in the daytime. At night when darkness falls everybody ought to praise God because of Brother Fire, through whom our eyes get light at night time.

For all of us are, as it were, blind, and the Lord with these two brothers of ours gives light to our eyes. For them in particular, and for all the creatures, we ought to praise the Creator.—Words of Saint Francis, from *The Mirror of Perfection*

### Notes

[1] *Rule of 1221, Omnibus,* p. 50.

[2] *Legend of Perugia, Omnibus,* pp. 1020-1021.

[3] Eloi Leclerc, *The Canticle of the Creatures, Symbols of Union* (Chicago: Franciscan Herald Press, 1970).

# Deepening Your Acquaintance

## Portiuncula

*On the plain below Assisi stands the basilica of St. Mary of the Angels. It was built in 1569 to protect the "birthplace" of the Franciscan Order, the Portiuncula, or "Little Portion," one of the churches Francis repaired with his own hands. Francis and his brothers lived in mud huts close to this beloved chapel. Francis died here in 1226; a small reliquary contains his bandages and cord. Huge crowds of pilgrims flock to this spot for a plenary indulgence given on August 2, the anniversary of the chapel's dedication.*

As you make your journey down the hill from Assisi to the new city of St. Mary of the Angels where you began your pilgrimage/retreat, you see the giant basilica of Our Lady of the Angels hovering over the tiny church of the Portiuncula, like a mother protecting a frail child, shielding it from wind and cold, literally putting herself between it and any threatening adversary. Almost womb-like, the basilica has nurtured the Portiuncula's life for hundreds of years. Without the mothering basilica over the top of it, the little chapel, completely encapsulated on the main floor, would have crumbled away from exposure to the elements or, perhaps worse, nakedness before human schemes.

When you arrive here on your last stop before

returning to the train station, having now come full circle, you sense the holiness of this place, perhaps because more than any other Franciscan shrine or church, it was part of the life and the death of Saint Francis. It is not hard to imagine that this was the center of his dream.

As a young man Francis caught fish to pay the yearly rent of one basketful to the Benedictines. Here the brothers, with the forest close about them, sang their evening compline; their praises echoed up the mountainside to Clare and her sisters and the people inside Assisi's walls. Here their small cooking fires dotted the forest clearing, a witness to the city and travelers—the brothers' hearts were warmed and inflamed by the fire of love.

Here Brothers Leo, Angelo, Bernard, Rufino, Sylvester and others were taught to beg and to cry and to laugh in ecstasy, and to share—painfully at times—the reality of their empty stomachs and aching limbs. Here Brother Juniper joyously danced, throwing this and that into a grand fiasco of a soup to greet his brothers' return—but also to diminish their supplies and remind them of their call to simplicity and their commitment not to provide for the future. And here Francis and the brothers received Clare and Pacifica, clothing them with the habit of Lady Poverty. Here Francis died.

And now you, pilgrim, have returned to this place on the plain below Assisi. It is now but a short walk to the train station where your pilgrimage-retreat began. A short walk, but long, perhaps, in time, if you stop to see what has fallen by the road; if you respond with love to what you see; if you care in a practical way for what you see; if you commit yourself to building a community that will provide sustained assistance. You may be in your soul's Umbria a long time. You have only to follow your pilgrim heart.

## Resources About Francis and Clare of Assisi

### Books

Bodo, Murray, O.F.M. *Clare, A Light in the Garden*, revised and expanded edition. Cincinnati, Ohio: St. Anthony Messenger Press, 1992.

_____. *Francis: The Journey and the Dream*, revised edition. Cincinnati, Ohio: St Anthony Messenger Press, 1988.

_____. *Tales of St. Francis: Ancient Stories for Contemporary Living*. Cincinnati, Ohio: St. Anthony Messenger Press, 1992.

_____. *Through the Year With Francis of Assisi: Daily Meditations From His Words and Life*. Cincinnati, Ohio: St. Anthony Messenger Press, 1993.

_____. *The Way of St. Francis: The Challenge of Franciscan Spirituality for Everyone*. Cincinnati, Ohio: St. Anthony Messenger Press, 1995.

Boff, Leonardo. *Saint Francis: A Model for Human Liberation*. New York: Crossroad, 1985.

Carney, Margaret, O.S.F. *The First Franciscan Woman*. Quincy, Ill.: Franciscan Press, 1993.

Chesterton, G.K. *St. Francis of Assisi*. New York: Doubleday and Co., Image Books, 1957.

*Clare of Assisi: Early Documents*, ed. and trans. Regis Armstrong, O.F.M. Cap. New York: Paulist Press, 1988.

De Robeck, Nesta. *Saint Clare of Assisi*. Chicago, Ill.: Franciscan Herald Press, 1980.

Englebert, Omer. *Saint Francis of Assisi*. Chicago, Ill.: Franciscan Herald Press, 1965.

Fortini, Arnaldo. *Francis of Assisi*. New York: Crossroad, 1981.

*Francis and Clare: The Complete Works*, ed. and trans. Regis Armstrong, O.F.M. Cap., and Ignatius C. Brady, O.F.M. New York: Paulist Press, 1982.

Green, Julien. *God's Fool: The Life and Times of Francis of Assisi*. San Francisco: Harper and Row, 1985.

Habig, Marion, O.F.M., ed. *Francis of Assisi: Omnibus of Sources*. Quincy, Ill.: Franciscan Press, 1972.

Jorgensen, Johannes. *St. Francis of Assisi*. New York: Doubleday and Co., Image Books, 1955.

Kazantzakis, Nikos. *Saint Francis* (novel). New York: Simon and Schuster, 1962.

Miller, Ramona, O.S.F. *In the Footsteps of St. Clare: Pilgrim's Guide Book*. St. Bonaventure, New York: Franciscan Institute, 1993.

Normile, Patti. *Following Francis: A Spirituality for Daily Living*. Cincinnati: St. Anthony Messenger Press, 1996.

Peterson, Ingrid, O.S.F. *St. Clare of Assisi, A Biographical Study*. Quincy, Ill.: Franciscan Press, 1993.

Roggen, Heribert. *The Spirit of St. Clare*. Chicago, Ill.: Franciscan Herald Press, 1971.

Saint Sing, Susan. *St. Francis: Poet of Creation*. Chicago, Ill.: Franciscan Herald Press, 1985.

Seraphim, Mary, P.C.P.A. *Clare: Her Light and Her Song*. Chicago, Ill.: Franciscan Herald Press, 1984.

**Videos**

Hodgson, Karen Lee. *Clare of Assisi*. Clare Productions, Oblate Media and Communication Corporation, 1994.

Sbicca, Arturo. *St. Clare of Assisi*. Distributed by St. Anthony Messenger Press, Cincinnati, Ohio, 1993.

Sbicca, Arturo. *St. Francis of Assisi*. Distributed by St. Anthony Messenger Press, Cincinnati, Ohio, 1992.

Zeffirelli, Franco. *Brother Sun, Sister Moon*. Paramount Communications Co., 1972.